THE ALTRUISTIC CAPITALIST

HOW TO LEAD FOR PURPOSE AND PROFIT

LYNN YAP

NDP

NEW DEGREE PRESS

THE ALTRUISTIC CAPITALIST

How to Lead for Purpose and Profit

ISBN   978-1-63676-862-5 *Paperback*

978-1-63730-180-7 *Kindle Ebook*

978-1-63730-306-1 *Ebook*

THE ALTRUISTIC CAPITALIST

ESPECIALLY FOR NINA

" A RISING TIDE LIFTS ALL BOATS" -JOHN F KENNEDY

WITH ALL MY VERY BEST

For my parents, who showed me that it is never
too late to learn how to build doll houses.

CONTENTS

————

FROM SPARKS
TO A FLAME

———

I was not at my grandmother's bedside as she lay dying. I missed saying goodbye to my only living grandparent in her final hours. I did not even attend her funeral due to work.

It was May 2012. I was working on Facebook's initial public offering (IPO). With the economy fresh from the wake of the financial crisis of 2008, the deal was the largest tech IPO at the time. It raised $16 billion. On the first day of trading, Facebook's market capitalization ballooned to $90 billion, launching the then-eight-year-old startup into the realm of other technology giants such as Amazon and Google.[1]

Every investment bank, including mine, wanted a piece of the action. We wanted the fat fees from underwriting a transaction of this size. Working on a deal like this would give us bragging rights for future deals. Everyone wanted their

---

1   Figures are as of Friday May 18, 2012 from Yahoo Finance.

name on the S-1 cover, which lists all the deal's underwriting investment banks. [2] My team had courted and cajoled Facebook for two years. When they told us we had earned a place on the S-1 cover, we were elated.

Toward the end of April, shortly before the roadshow for the IPO, my grandmother's health took a turn for the worse. [3] She had been ill for a while, and the doctors feared that she would not survive for more than a few weeks. I lived in New York, and my grandmother was in Malaysia, a twenty-four-hour flight away.

My life in investment banking was grueling. I worked eighty to a hundred hours a week. I spent Sundays catching up on the news from Friday night and preparing for the next day's meetings. I missed many birthdays, weddings, and holidays with family and friends in those years. When my grandmother fell ill, I had not been home to see her for two years.

"I would like to take some time off to go to Malaysia to see my grandmother," I nervously told my manager.

Without skipping a beat, he responded, "You can't go."

"She is quite sick, and the doctors think she won't make it," I tried again, less confidently.

---

2   The U.S. Securities and Exchange Commission (SEC) requires companies that want to raise money from the public on a national exchange in the US to file an S-1 registration form.

3   A roadshow is a series of presentations made to investors conducted prior to the IPO itself.

"Look, Facebook is going to go on the road any day now. We can't risk you not being around to make sure that everything goes smoothly," he explained.

I felt conflicted. I was torn between my duty to my family and my commitment to my work. I was the only one on the ground to ensure a smooth execution of the deal. I'd worked hard on it. Yet what other sacrifices on my family or myself would the business ask me to make in the future?

In the end, I bowed to the pressure and stayed in New York. Facebook started its two-week roadshow, and my grandmother passed away. I felt ashamed and weak for not pushing back and not standing up for myself. We could have asked someone to take over in my absence, but we didn't even discuss the option.

AWAKENING

Not long after that, I decided to leave my investment banking career. Facebook was the last deal I worked on. I gained much experience in the financial markets and business. But nowhere in the rows of financial data did we talk about business's impact on people and the planet. We don't see how a company directly affects the lives of its employees on the balance sheet. We talk about cause and effect, but the effect of business on the environment and community is invisible on the profit and loss statement.

My conversations with peers and coworkers revealed their frustrations at work. A few worried about their job stability when automation would make them redundant. Analytical work and repetitive tasks will be done faster with artificial intelligence, and natural language processing. They felt helpless because the company did not invest in training them to transition into other types of work when those innovations inevitably came knocking at the door.

Some felt powerless in their organizations because leaders fixed their mindsets and practices on growing sales and profits without considering the human cost to their employees, customers, or the community. They felt handcuffed to do things the old way because of entrenched mindsets, processes, and organizational structures.

Many wanted to give back. They did not see the connection of how their daily work, making beautiful presentations or spending hours with spreadsheets, contributed to society. Others struggled to find time outside of work and family commitments to volunteer.

I invested time in projects that created a positive impact in the community. I built a leadership and training program to encourage girls' participation in computer science and mathematics in school. We partnered with companies to provide mentors for the students. We met with human resources, marketing, and strategy executives who got excited when they heard the details. They understood the benefits. This program and others like it increased employee engagement and re-ignited their passion at work.

When I worked with various adidas teams on sustainability-focused innovations, people on the projects seemed to work harder and walk taller. They saw the impact of the work they were doing and became strong advocates of the products they created. They bragged to their friends and family, which attracted future employee candidates. No ad is more powerful than word of mouth from someone you know.

These projects also attracted public attention and new customers. Both new and existing customers reported a higher intent to purchase these innovations compared to other non-sustainability-focused products coming down the pipeline. Customers paid a premium for sustainability, and these products sold quickly during their launch.

I also worked with an adidas team to develop a measurement framework to analyze the impact of a company's actions on its community. We debated over questions including direct and indirect impacts, intended and unintended consequences, and different complexities around data collection. This helped me understand the type of activities that move the needle in solving social issues. Sending gifts once a year to the local orphanage is nice, but it does not address the orphan's needs for mentorship and care. I also learned the importance of coordination across the value chain to address the cause, rather than symptoms, of the problem. Collaboration can also scale and faster implement innovative solutions on social issues.

In addition to stronger relationships with employees and the customer base, one study found businesses that are a force for good did better than their peers by 10.5 times on a financial basis.[4] Doing good is good for business. At the height of

---

4   Tony Schwartz, "Companies That Practice *Conscious Capitalism* Perform 10x Better," *Harvard Business Review*, April 4, 2013.

COVID-19, investors moved their money to sustainability funds, and these financial assets outperformed traditional funds and indices.[5] To reduce operational disruption and unlock opportunities for savings and efficiencies, leaders can proactively manage their supply chain for longer-term shifts in climate and poor labor conditions.[6]

Employees, customers, and investors' interests are starting to converge. Each stakeholder wants businesses to be more inclusive of all their interests. The tide is turning for sustainable long-term growth. We increasingly realize we need to press the reset button for value creation—we can't maximize for profit alone.

CATALYST

I felt compelled to write about how leaders can mobilize their teams in the wake of COVID-19. During the pandemic, I saw how quickly companies came together to provide necessary personal protective equipment. Public and private organizations collaborated to produce an effective vaccine in record time. It started me thinking about how much we could achieve if businesses, governmental agencies, and nonprofit organizations came together to solve environmental problems and social issues at scale.

At the same time, employees and communities grew vocal about their unhappiness and grievances at work. Journalists

---

5   Jon Hale, "Sustainable Equity Funds Outperform Traditional Peers in 2020," *Morningstar,* January 8, 2021.

6   Tensie Whelan and Carly Fink, "The Comprehensive Business Case for Sustainability," *Harvard Business Review*, October 21, 2016.

uncovered business practices that exacerbated the growing disparity in income and employment. It was no longer enough to talk the talk; companies needed to step up and walk the talk.

My personal experiences showed me that leaders did not always know how to walk the talk. After many years of prioritizing growth and aggressively cutting expenses, they did not always know how to shift their business to become a force for good. Leaders needed a new mindset to humanize business.

Change starts with leaders. Leaders see a vision, start a movement, and bring others along with them. Within business, leaders set ambitions around purpose and start the chain reaction of movement and progress in the teams around them. They role model behavior that will energize others to take action. Other elements needed to realize the ambitions will follow: culture, strategy, incentives, organizational structure, and processes. All will shift according to the purpose.

I developed the **Altruistic Capitalist Mindset** from my observations of and interviews with leaders who led profitable and sustainable businesses. These leaders inspired others to take action, grew a loyal customer base, retained an engaged workforce, and provided investors with strong financial returns.

They are different from leaders of the past when public perception was that business had to maximize for profit. Perspectives and expectations have evolved. So managing business purely by numbers without understanding the humanity behind those figures can't work in the future.

Unlike other books, *The Altruistic Capitalist* promotes "alpha" and "beta" traits. Business leaders need to measure their progress with data and listen actively for feedback. When designing solutions, look at the facts and rigorously test assumptions. At the same time, intentionally develop trustworthy relationships with others and share knowledge.

This book benefited from interviews with entrepreneurs and executives of global companies located in the US, UK, and Europe. Their stories are counter-balanced with research and surveys to verify hypotheses. As much as possible, I tried to reduce blind spots and develop a robust tool kit to enable leaders to make the shift.

When leaders and entrepreneurs shift their mindset and adopt some of the practices outlined in this book, they can create a flourishing work environment of engaged employees. This does not mean discarding financial savviness or strategy. But strategy and business model need to be examined through a social and environmental lens. The Altruistic Capitalist Mindset can help leaders galvanize their team. Leaders can transform from short-term transactional thinking to thinking in the business of relationships with their employees, customers, vendors, and investors while protecting the environment.

THE ALTRUISTIC CAPITALIST MINDSET
Part 1 of the book identifies the macro trends that point toward a more humane form of capitalism. It discusses the perspective change that we need to make when thinking

about business, governments, and nonprofit organizations in solving social causes. We will also look at how conventional leadership ideas will not work when we are in the business of relationships. Relationships require trust and long-term thinking to succeed.

Part 2 dives into the Altruistic Capitalist Mindset that consists of three mini-mindsets: **mindfulness, curiosity,** and **grit**. First, the monk personifies mindfulness. Mindfulness clarifies purpose and core values to balance the interests of different business stakeholders. This becomes critical when there are no obvious answers.

Second, the five-year-old personifies curiosity. When leaders embed curiosity that leads to learning in their business, their teams will design more innovative solutions. In times of rapid change and uncertainty, this mindset increases organizational resilience and business stability.

Third, athletes are about grit. When we adopt the habits of athletes, we can go the distance to achieve our goals. Although we emphasize teamwork in the office, many organizations become stuck in their silo departments after passing a specific size. I don't see how we can operate as lone wolves in an interconnected world without sharing knowledge and helping each other through prosperous and challenging times.

In each mini-mindset chapter, I will share practices from leaders who scale these mindsets in their organizations. Each chapter ends with a **Reflect** section with questions I hope will spark ideas in igniting a shift toward the Altruistic Capitalist Mindset.

I believe the lessons I share in this book will reframe how we lead businesses. The Altruistic Capitalist Mindset combined with a sound business model and strategy can enable companies to reach their highest potential for the benefit of all their stakeholders. I hope the stories will help you reimagine what is possible and cultivate a more purpose-driven and impactful ecosystem.

PART I

CURRENT STATE

*The forces of a capitalist society, if left unchecked,
tend to make the rich richer and the poor poorer.*

JAWAHARLAL NEHRU

CHAPTER 1

LAW OF THE JUNGLE
OF CAPITALISM

———

"DON'T BUY THIS JACKET"

In *The New York Times*' Black Friday issue, bursting with door-busting sales flyers, the ad's headline was more than bold. It was downright audacious.

Patagonia, the American outdoor clothing retailer behind the ad, placed a photo of one of their popular jackets under the headline. Not the image of a competitor's product, but one of their own.

It was Black Friday, 2011—the day after the Thanksgiving holiday—traditionally the busiest shopping day of the year in the US. Historically, Black Friday kicked off the holiday shopping season, the five-week period during which retailers rang in enough sales to bring their books out of the red (losses) to end the year in the black (profits).

The ad challenged would-be shoppers to consider the impact of their consumption behavior on the planet. It listed the environmental cost of producing the jacket: 135 liters of water used and twenty pounds of carbon dioxide emitted.

Five years later, Rose Marcario, the CEO, declared that Patagonia would donate 100 percent of global sales achieved on Black Friday that year to grassroots organizations working on protecting the environment. She expected $2 million in sales.[7] Her estimate was way off. Patagonia reported a single-day record of $10 million (and, as promised, donated all of it).

According to Marcario, "The initiative attracted thousands who had never purchased anything from Patagonia before ... making buying decisions that align with strong environmental values—and taking steps to get more directly involved."[8]

A year later, Patagonia, under the leadership of Marcario, joined a coalition of Native American and grassroots groups and sued the United States Government and former US President Donald Trump. Former President Trump had proclaimed to reduce the Bears Ears National Monument and Grand Staircase-Escalante National Monument by 85 percent and 50 percent, respectively.[9] The lands are protected Native American sites, designated to preserve the heritage, history, and art of five different tribes. They are also popular

7   "100 Percent Today, 1 Percent Every Day," Patagonia, accessed January 29, 2021.

8   "Record-breaking Black Friday Sales to Benefit the Planet," Patagonia, accessed January 29, 2021.

9   Rose Marcario, "Patagonia CEO: This Is Why We're Suing President Trump," *Time*, December 6, 2017.

sites for outdoor climbing. The loss of these lands as national monuments would mean opening up the locations to oil and gas leasing.

These stories tell how Marcario, a former finance professional, went against conventional business wisdom. She chose to participate in expensive litigation instead of hoarding capital. She chose to give away money to nonprofit organizations instead of returning it to shareholders. She balanced competing for market share and growth with other retailers and telling customers not to buy her company's products to reduce consumption. How do we explain her decisions?

THE SOCIAL RESPONSIBILITY OF BUSINESS

Capitalism is an economic system characterized by the free market. The market's supply and demand forces dictate the level of production of goods and services (and distribution of incomes) rather than central government planning.

Milton Friedman, Nobel Prize winner in Economic Science, was a big believer in the free market. The least intervention from the government, the better. He claimed that "There is one and only one social responsibility of business—to use its resources and engage in activities designed to increase its profits so long as it stays within the rules of the game, which is to say, engages in open and free competition without deception fraud." [10]

---

10   Milton Friedman, "A Friedman Doctrine - The Social Responsibility of Business Is to Increase Its Profits," *The New York Times*, September 13, 1970.

The corporate executive, an agent to the shareholders, is directly responsible to them. Their responsibility is to maximize profits within the laws and ethical customs of society. This concept is widely known as **shareholder capitalism**.

Critics of shareholder capitalism believe the focus on investors lead business to prioritize short-term gains and cut corners and costs. Some companies try to create monopolies in the market, leading to increased earnings and power concentrated in few industry players. Rana Foroohar argued that large companies increasingly act like banks through financial hedging and tax optimization to maximize profits instead of creating long-term value for employees and customers.[11]

Investors expect the corporate executive to return profits to them and increase growth. So instead of investing in innovation and employee development, executives devise other ways to please shareholders. This situation is particularly acute in public companies. Shareholder activists pressure business leaders to buy back their shares that increase the stock price and return the money to the shareholders in a tax-efficient manner. This value extraction from business enriches the rich investor to the detriment of the common consumer and employee. Eventually, this leads to economic stagnation. When employees are not trained to keep up with new technology, businesses experience employment instability and income inequality.

---

11   Rana Foroohar, *Makers and Takers: How Wall Street Destroyed Main Street* (Crown Business, 2016).

Shareholder capitalism tells the executive to ignore the business impact on the environment and the community they operate in. Like it or not, all businesses have an environmental impact, either through the resources it uses or the waste it produces. The presence of a company also changes the community's fabric, from the jobs they create (or destroy) to social mobility and cohesion.

The alternative solution is **stakeholder capitalism**. Business is responsible to all stakeholders alike, not just shareholders. The corporate executive must consider the interests of employees, vendors, customers, the environment, and investors, focusing on maximum value creation. This model requires business to take the long-term view; there are no shortcuts to achieving job satisfaction, fair trade and safe environmental practices, and sustainable investor returns.

As we will see later in the chapter, the business community has yet to embrace stakeholder capitalism fully. Juggling the stakeholders' competing priorities is a delicate balancing act, and real progress will take time. The corporate executive needs to shift their perspective and mindset to succeed in stakeholder capitalism.

DISTRUST IN CAPITALISM

The free market is like a machine-learning robot. It gets smarter and better as more information is fed into it. Oversupply of a product reduces the product price, telling the producer to stop producing. Advocates for capitalism argue that this results in capitalist economies having higher income levels, lower poverty, and higher life expectancy than socialist nations.[12]

Millennials, those born between 1981 and 1996, started to distrust capitalism during the financial crisis of 2008. They believe that greed, characteristic of capitalism, is causing the growing income inequality gap.[13] As many as 56 percent believed that capitalism in its current form is doing more harm than good in the world. In most markets, less than half of the mass population trust their institutions to do what is right.[14]

A Harvard University survey found 51 percent of American millennials were against capitalism.[15] Similarly, in the UK, YouGov, an international analytics and research company, reported that two-thirds of Britons believed capitalism increases inequality. More than 70 percent believed that big business cheated its way to success.[16]

But the problem is not capitalism or free markets itself. Millennials are actually concerned about the rise of power by large enterprises.[17] As many as 83 percent believe that too

12   "Economic Freedom of the World: 2020 Annual Report," Fraser Institute, accessed January 29, 2021.
13   Michael Dimock, "Defining Generations: Where Millennials End and Generation Z Begins," Pew Research Center, accessed January 29, 2021.
14   "2020 Trust Barometer," Edelman, January 19, 2020.
15   Max Ehrenfreund, "A Majority of Millennials Now Reject Capitalism, Poll Shows," *The Washington Post*, April 26, 2016.
16   Sam Coates, "Verdict on Capitalism: Unfair and Corrupt," *The Times*, November 3, 2015.
17   Lydia Saad, "Socialism as Popular as Capitalism among Young Adults in U.S.," *Gallup*, November 25, 2019.

much power is concentrated in the hands of a few.[18] They blame the bottom-line devoted baby boomers for writing policies that made the rich richer and the poor poorer. "The disintegration of the social safety net created by unions, pensions, health care and affordable tuition has been accompanied by ... a collapse of the psychological safety net" for millennials.[19] Their perception of growing inequity and unfairness in the system caused their distrust of big business.

THE GIG ECONOMY

As many of us hunkered down and worked from home during COVID-19 in 2020, we came to recognize the unsung heroes in our labor markets. They stocked our shelves, delivered our food and Amazon orders, cleaned our hospitals, and cared for the old and vulnerable. They were likely to be overworked and underpaid. The physical requirement for their manual work meant higher exposure to the virus. If they got ill, they could lose their incomes because there is little job security for their work.

Others at the bottom of the economic pyramid also lacked security. They were more likely to lose their jobs, experience pay cuts, and have trouble paying their bills due to the pandemic.[20] Millions of hospitality workers (restaurants, travel,

---

18 John P. Banks, "Millennials and the Future of Electric Utilities," *Brookings, Planet Policy* (blog), July 11, 2014.

19 Joshua Coleman, "What Boomers Can Learn from Millennials about Changing the World — and Their Relationships," *NBC News,* March 2, 2021.

20 Kim Parker, Rachel Minkin, and Jesse Bennett, "Economic Fallout From COVID-19 Continues to Hit Lower-Income Americans the Hardest," Pew Research Center, September 24, 2020.

hotels) lost their jobs and the ability to support themselves and their families.

Although governments intervened and provided COVID-19 relief payments, these were often not enough. Some who lost their jobs turned to gig work with companies such as Deliveroo and Instacart, which experienced increased demand for their services to deliver food or groceries. This consequence can be expected; at times of low employment, workers will use gig work to supplement their income or savings.

COVID-19 pushed others to freelance on digital platforms such as Upwork and Fiverr to offer their skills for contractual pay. These platforms were lifesavers for designers, software developers, or product specialists who lost their full-time jobs at companies. Similarly, for companies forced to cut costs and downsize their teams, these platforms provided less costly on-demand labor to operate their business.

Gig workers and freelancers are cheaper for employers because they don't have minimum wage and health benefits like full-time employees. Without the protection that employees receive, gig workers and freelancers tend to be underpaid and overworked. Companies don't want these workers on their books because the company would pay more taxes and expenses. They see no financial incentive to change their business model for contractual workers.

If the proportion of gig workers increases in the economy and they receive no protection or benefits from their gig employers, we will see further income inequality in the market. An increase in gig labor supply will decrease their ability to command a reasonable value for their work as the market competes on price. Without the cushion of protection from minimum wage and other benefits, their effective take-home pay would be less, creating a gap between the "executive" and the gig worker.

MAKING MONEY

Even though we see problems with the capitalist system, there is no need to throw the baby out with the bathwater.

As we saw earlier with Patagonia, Marcario used her leadership position to use business as a force for good. She challenged the community to look "at business through a more holistic lens other than profit … (because) profit isn't the only measure of success."[21]

She left her illustrious finance career because she was tired of the rich only interested in lining their own pockets and serving themselves.[22] She felt devoid of purpose at work.

Just as others questioned profit maximization by Friedman, Marcario questioned the practice of making decisions based on meeting quarterly reporting targets at public companies. She argued, "If you're making decisions based on meeting your earnings-per-share number and not about the long-term health of your company, its employees, the environment, and the community you're operating in, then you're probably making a decision that isn't good for the long term … the

---

21   Drake Baer, "Patagonia CEO: 'There's No Way I Should Make One Decision Based on Quarterly Results,'" *Business Insider,* November 19, 2014.

22   Rose Marcario, "Sand Mandalas & Goodbyes," *LinkedIn,* June 17, 2020.

whole system is built around metrics and a process that is not healthy for people and the planet."[23]

But this did not mean that she thought capitalism was wrong. Instead, "capitalism needs to evolve to consider more than a shareholder and a quarterly earnings report" and to serve multiple stakeholders.[24]

The Business Roundtable agreed with this view.[25] The organization had consistently endorsed profit maximization and supported Friedman since 1997. However, in August 2019, 181 CEOs pledged to benefit all stakeholders in their business.[26] All stakeholders meant employees, suppliers, customers, communities, the environment, and shareholders. This indicates the start in the business shift away from a focus on profits to a value-creation and impact maximization model.

Marcario was an example of an **Altruistic Capitalist**. She believed in competition, which encourages innovation in the market. She would challenge her team and ask them, "How do we make it uncomfortable for other businesses not to follow us?"[27] In fact, she raised the bar for herself, her team, and her competitors when she changed Patagonia's mission

---

23 Drake Baer, "Patagonia CEO: 'There's No Way I Should Make One Decision Based on Quarterly Results'," *Business Insider,* November 19, 2014.

24 Jenna Garden, "Rose Marcario: Environmentalism Is for Everyone," Insights by Stanford Business, June 1, 2020.

25 The Business Roundtable Is an Organization of CEOs of Leading U.S. Companies, Focused on Promoting a Thriving U.S. Economy.

26 "Business Roundtable Redefines the Purpose of a Corporation to Promote 'An Economy That Serves All Americans'," Business Roundtable, August 19, 2019.

27 "How These Leading CEOs Use Questions to Drive Success," MIT Sloan, November 8, 2018.

statement from "Do no unnecessary harm" to "We're in the business to save our home planet."

Marcario leveraged her private equity and finance experience to streamline the supply chain and launch strategic initiatives that propelled Patagonia's business.[28] Tin Shed Ventures, the corporate venture fund of Patagonia, diversifies the company's revenue source. The fund also gives the company a front-row seat to innovations in sustainable materials and other technologies to support product development.

Worn Wear and Action Works display Marcario's ability to use technology to grow Patagonia's business and increase customer engagement. Worn Wear is an e-commerce platform to extend a garment's life. Customers can repair and recycle their Patagonia products or purchase used Patagonia products on Worn Wear. The platform has the double benefit of reducing consumption and landfill and reducing Patagonia's reliance on selling new products.

Action Works brings Patagonia's customers and the grassroots organizations they work with together online. Customers can volunteer and donate to organizations working on causes that they feel most passionate about. Marcario built this digital ecosystem because this deepens relationships between Patagonia and its customers. It is no longer a transactional relationship of buying and selling a product. When the customers invest in more touchpoints with the brand, they become more loyal and engaged.

---

28 Jeff Beer, "EXCLUSIVE: Patagonia CEO Rose Marcario Is Stepping Down," *Fast Company, June* 10, 2020.

These initiatives demonstrate Marcario's financial rigor and creativity in leading a for-profit business. The stories at the start of the chapter demonstrate the practicing Buddhist's ability to act as a purpose-driven leader in standing up for causes important to her and the business.

When Marcario stepped down as CEO in June 2020, she had quadrupled its revenue and made Patagonia a billion-dollar company.[29] Patagonia's bold moves did make their competitors uncomfortable, and other apparel retailers have started to transform their supply chain to address their respective environmental footprints. Mammoths such as H&M and Kering launched initiatives to repurpose garments and publish sustainability reports in response.[30] The company also boasts strong employee retention, with only a turnover rate of 4 percent compared to 13 percent among other retailers. Stepping up to defend causes you believe in reaps financial benefits.

THE BOTTOM LINE

- Milton Friedman's theory of shareholder primacy has pervaded much of business thinking. In perfect free markets, the corporate executive's sole responsibility is to maximize profit (unless otherwise stated by the shareholders).
- Millennials distrust capitalism and profit maximization, which they believe has led to the growing income inequality in society.

---

29 Jeff Beer, "EXCLUSIVE: Patagonia CEO Rose Marcario Is Stepping Down," *Fast Company*, June 10, 2020.

30 Limei Hong, "Patagonia's Circular Economy Strategy," *Business of Fashion*, January 17, 2017.

- Emerging shifts in the workforce have led to the rise of the gig economy, leaving gig workers and freelancers without a safety net of stability and minimum wage protection. This could exacerbate the growing income inequality problem.
- Rose Marcario, the former CEO at Patagonia, is an Altruistic Capitalist. She exercised financial discipline and fiercely protected the environment. She practiced stakeholder capitalism, which balances the interests of all stakeholders: employees, suppliers, customers, investors, and the environment.
- The next chapter examines the responsibility and accountability behind social and environmental issues.

REFLECT

1. What are the advantages and disadvantages of shareholder primacy?
2. What are the potential challenges of implementing stakeholder capitalism?
3. How might we evolve the current model of capitalism?
4. In addition to the shift to the gig economy, what other trends could worsen inequality (income, gender, race)?
5. Apart from Patagonia, what other businesses practice stakeholder capitalism?

CHAPTER 2

WHOSE JOB IS IT?

———

Before COVID-19 temporarily restricted in-person events, I was waiting in the conference room at the start of an artificial intelligence event. I scanned the room to see if I recognized anyone.

It was the usual crowd of T-shirts and jeans, more than a smattering of hoodies, and a buffet of facial hairstyles—a sea of black, gray, and dark blue attired men.

Then I spotted a female figure. My inner self heaved a small sigh of relief. I was not the only woman in this room.

When I worked in innovation and technology, I was often the only woman in the room. I also stood out because I was an expatriate and a minority. Older Caucasian men in these conversations often had different perspectives from me, and sometimes I strained to get them to see my point of view.

Although women make up half the labor force, they account for less than 30 percent of science-related professionals.[31]

———

31   "Women in Science, Fact Sheet No 55," UNESCO, June 2019.

Women make up only 22 percent of artificial intelligence professionals (AI), and in machine learning, 12 percent.[32]

Why does this matter?

AI will automate more and more of our roles. In the short and medium term, we expect women to face more disruption because of the disproportionate distribution of work roles across genders. For example, more women perform clerical and data entry-type tasks.[33] Unless we reskill these women, they risk losing their jobs.

In addition, today's underrepresentation of women in AI roles means that the unconscious biases of those implementing AI today may be baked into the tools with severe consequences in the future.

Any existing gender bias at the workplace, for instance, could be perpetuated and exacerbated over the long term. AI inherently learns from the data its developers provide the AI. If the data provided is biased, then the resulting algorithms and solutions would be biased too. This could lead to an even larger gender gap in the workplace.

We face a similar issue with the lower representation of ethnic minorities in AI professions, with the same consequence of systemizing unconscious bias. For example, when the AI model uses underlying data to grant loans, we may exclude

---

32   "The Global Gender Gap Report 2018," World Economic Forum, 2018.
33   "Will Robots Really Steal Our Jobs?" PWC, February 2018.

certain groups or neighborhoods based on statistical correlations. These models perpetuate unfair historical biases.

COVID-19 pushed companies to scale remote work rapidly, digitalize their business, and accelerate their automation initiatives.[34] It is estimated that 50 percent of all employees would need to be reskilled by 2025.[35]

But two-thirds of employers expect a return on their investment from reskilling within one year.[36] When employers need to reskill a large proportion of their workforce, one year is not enough time to transform their employees' skills into the ones they need. So most employers choose to hire experienced workers from the market rather than invest in training their existing workforce. Consequently, the labor market faces instability and a high rate of unemployment in certain groups.

HOUSE ON FIRE

We may have heard at least one older person complain, "Boy, it is so much hotter today than when I was growing up."

They wouldn't be wrong. The average global temperature has risen by 1.1 degrees Celsius (2 Fahrenheit) since 1880.[37] Our world getting warmer is mainly because of us. From burning fossil fuels to cutting down rainforests, human activities have increased greenhouse gases and caused global warming.

---

34 "The Future of Jobs Report 2020," World Economic Forum, October 20, 2020.

35 Ibid.

36 Ibid.

37 "World of Change: Global Temperatures," Earth Observatory, accessed January 29, 2021.

Some experts argue that the increase in global temperature causes more droughts and increases storm intensity. The more water is evaporated into the atmosphere, the more intense the storms. The warmer the atmosphere and sea temperatures, the faster the wind speeds in tropical storms.

The increase in the number and intensity of natural disasters has both an economic impact and a human toll. Reinsurer Munich Re reported 820 natural disasters in 2019, a number that has tripled since 1980. Hurricane Katrina cost the total insured market $40 billion.[38]

Who pays for the damage and loss suffered?

As with the loss of jobs due to automation, global warming and climate change are wicked problems. The term "wicked problems" was used to define difficult or impossible problems due to incomplete, contradictory, or changing information. In contrast, mathematics or puzzles are solvable because of the finite information given and the game's clear rules.

These problems are "wicked" because they tend to have many interdependencies. Changing one element could impact another stakeholder or cause another problem. It also means that you need diverse skill sets and knowledge to solve such problems.

Wicked problems impact multiple generations, and no single individual, organization, or solution can control the outcome.

---

38 "Munich Re Analyzes Katrina/Rita Impact; Insured Loss Around $40 Billion," *Insurance Journal*, September 28, 2005.

The United Nations (UN) published the Sustainable Development Goals (SDGs) in Rio de Janeiro in 2012. The UN identified critical social, economic, and environmental issues behind the SDGs that need to be solved by 2030. It was a universal call to action for public and private partnerships to protect the planet and ensure peace and prosperity for everyone.

RESPONSIBILITY AND ACCOUNTABILITY

In the past, the public expected governments and nonprofit organizations to tackle social and environmental issues. Governments were the most accountable because of their far-reaching influence over their citizens and with other countries. Corporate executives focused on maximizing profit, and the government intervened in industries through pollution and competition laws, for example, to regulate the market. During a financial crisis, governments have also intervened to bail out industries such as the banking industry and provide stimulus payments to support the economy.

The state also directed the economy through infrastructure projects, research and development, education, health care, and housing. This model keeps businesses in place to ensure that short-term interests do not outstrip societal benefits. State intervention has been critical in building strong economies, but it does not come without its own set of problems.

Corruption and favoritism lead to an unequal distribution of state contracts and arbitrary application of the law. The instability of ruling governments hinders progress in solving wicked problems. At times, we take one step forward only to be taken two steps back as governments flip-flop on policies based on who is in power.

Letting governments have the sole responsibility of tackling wicked problems doesn't seem to be the answer. While some of the tasks required to achieve the SDGs, such as implementing laws and providing certain public services fall within the government's purview, many of the tasks need technology, innovation, and collective action by multiple community players. Innovation often flourishes best with competition.

Governments also often arrive late to the game. Let's look at the SDG to reduce gender and income inequality. Governments can introduce discrimination laws to tackle this. But this is a backward-looking approach. Instead, businesses should take a proactive look at their policies and culture and take the necessary action to prevent discrimination and inequality in the first place.

For nonprofit organizations, funding is their main issue. Often, nonprofit groups are organized to treat the symptoms rather than the cause of wicked problems. These groups do not have the resources to design solutions and innovations that may intervene with how businesses and governments are run. This is a consequence of how these groups are set up and not the leadership's lack of intention.

Nonprofit organizations rely heavily on funding from government grants and individual and corporate donations. The funding structure of these organizations requires undue management time on fundraising and grant writing.

Managers of the nonprofit organizations spend the remainder of the time on the required oversight reporting. Grants are often short term, for example, three years, and for a stated purpose. Unless the nonprofit can secure long-term relationships, the organization can't make a dent in solving the problem. This is not to lessen the impact that nonprofit organizations make on alleviating the suffering of their beneficiaries. However, it is difficult to focus on implementing solutions that solve the root cause of wicked problems in the short term.

The cyclical state of its financing model creates instability in the nonprofit organization's operations. The nonprofit industry is subject to external financial market conditions. During recessions, when there is the highest need to provide for the weak and vulnerable, fewer funds are donated to nonprofit organizations. The lack of predictability in terms of the amount received and when the funds are received leads to difficulty in designing long-term solutions.

CORPORATE SOCIAL RESPONSIBILITY

This is not the first time in capitalist history that business leaders are called to step up. During the First Industrial Revolution, there was an increasing concern for employee working conditions, including long hours and child labor. The surge of coal and iron used in production caused pollution to rise.

Maybe we should take better care of our workers, the capitalists at the time thought.

One such capitalist was Robert Owen, a mill owner in New Lanark, Scotland. When he purchased the mill, living conditions were harsh. He improved housing, encouraged thrift and cleanliness, and focused on the children's education in the estate.

Owen even continued to pay the workers when the mill closed for four months during the War of 1812.[39] Even through this period and accounting for Owen's worker initiatives, the mill was profitable and respected by those who visited it.

Although Owen saw his workers' and the community's welfare as his responsibility as a business owner, corporate social responsibility (CSR) has only recently become mandatory for companies in some areas. In the 1990s, CSR standards were internationalized and CSR indices were published.

CSR teams at companies typically operate separately from the general business. They organize their activities around philanthropy and ethical policies. This includes donating to their cause of choice, partnering with nonprofit organizations, and doing local community work. At times, these activities seem more perfunctory, an afterthought of business leaders.

But this is not just about giving. We will not achieve the SDGs through public governance or donations alone. Many of the SDGs require a shift in how we organize ourselves and the way we do business. We need to:

---

39 *Encyclopedia Britannica Online*, Academic ed., s.v. "Robert Owen," accessed January 29, 2021.

- Decouple economic growth from environmental degradation
- Substantially reduce corruption and bribery
- Ensure responsive, inclusive, and representative decision-making at all levels

Since the time Friedman penned the article in 1970 on shareholder capitalism, public expectations have changed. It is no longer just the government and nonprofit organizations' responsibility to protect the vulnerable and the planet. The public now expects companies, public and private, to lead by example and shoulder responsibility for our society's wicked problems.

All businesses impact the environment, deplete resources, and, worse still, pollute the planet. We saw in Chapter 1 that the existing capitalism model ends up in inequality with economic power concentrated in a select few. If the profit-maximizing capitalists created the mess, shouldn't they be responsible for cleaning it up?

We know it is better to prevent a problem than deal with the ensuing damage. In the Altruistic Capitalist world, the business leader recognizes their social responsibility and embeds accountability in their companies' strategy, culture, and operations. Social and environmental problems are not just the burden of public and nonprofit agencies.

The Altruistic Capitalist has an active role to play in accomplishing the SDGs.

THE BOTTOM LINE

- Emerging innovations in artificial intelligence and global warming are examples of social and environmental issues that will cause instability in the near future. These are "wicked problems": problems that contain many interdependencies and are difficult to solve.
- In the past, we expected governments and nonprofit organizations to tackle wicked problems. However, both these constituents have their limitations.
- Public perception of the responsibility of business has evolved. They expect companies to shoulder their share of responsibility to drive the agenda forward on wicked problems.
- Next, we look at the legacy leadership mindset under profit maximization and what needs to evolve with business.

REFLECT

1. Choose a company (it may be your own business or the company you work with). What is the most critical wicked problem this company needs to solve? Why?
2. Who are the most important stakeholders who need to be involved in solving this problem? What is each of their roles and responsibilities?
3. What has been done so far? What has worked? What could be improved?
4. What more could be done?
5. What one small step could be taken today to impact this problem?

CHAPTER 3

WHO IS IN CHARGE?

———

Remember when your CEO told you to "Have a great f***ing time" in an email?

If you worked in Uber in 2013, you would. Travis Kalanick, then CEO of Uber, emailed his employees to talk about an upcoming company outing. The tone hinted at a culture based on excess and sexism.[40]

Kalanick and his cofounders were once the darlings of Silicon Valley. Uber's value proposition was to reduce the direct transportation market's supply gap.[41] The company matched private car owners with people who needed to get somewhere, facilitating car sharing at an affordable price.

Uber uses a dynamic price model, called surge pricing, to price car rides. Car rides become more expensive when demand is

---

40 Kara Swisher and Johana Bhuiyan "Uber CEO Kalanick Advised Employees on Sex Rules for a Company Celebration in 2013 'Miami letter'," *Vox*, June 8, 2017.

41 David Larcker and Brian Tayan, "Governance Gone Wild: Epic Misbehavior at Uber Technologies," *Stanford Closer Look Series*, October 11, 2017.

high and supply is low. Dynamic pricing incentivizes more drivers to head toward busy areas and car riders or customers to wait or be prepared to pay for the premium.

Kalanick wanted to win and took many risks. He expanded aggressively to dominate the ride-sharing industry. Less than four years after launching the Uber ride-hailing app, the company's reach had spread to 250 cities in fifty-three countries.

This "growth above all else" mindset led to disaster.[42]

Sexism was widespread at the company. Female employees complained of sexual harassment and discrimination. When Susan Fowler started working at Uber, her new manager propositioned her for sex over the work chat function. She reported the incident to the Human Resources team, who told her that her abuser was a "high performer." The HR team did not take any action against him except to give him a stern talking to. [43]

Waymo, the self-driving car business under Google, sued Uber for stealing intellectual property. It alleged that one of its employees, Anthony Levandowski, downloaded fourteen thousand files from Google before he left to start his own self-driving car business. Months later, Uber purchased Levandowski's startup.[44] At the time, there was a race as to who could build the first self-driving car.

---

42 Ibid.

43 Susan Fowler, "Reflecting on One Very, Very Strange Year at Uber," *Susan Fowler* (blog), February 19, 2017.

44 Daisuke Wakabayashi and Mike Isaac, "Google Self-Driving Car Unit Accuses Uber of Using Stolen Technology," *New York Times*, February 23, 2017.

In one more cunning act, the company allegedly used a software tool called Greyball, which would enable it to sidestep law enforcement. The software allows Uber to identify and circumvent officials trying to clamp down on the ride-hailing service. The tool had started as a way to prevent competitors from finding the location of Uber's drivers. Used for both these reasons, Greyball was a tactic to increase the company's monopoly in the market.

These mistakes and others prompted a #DeleteUber campaign. More than two hundred thousand users did precisely that in a single weekend—delivering a market boost to its competitor, Lyft.

Kalanick prioritized profit to the exclusion of everything else. He was opportunistic and had no scruples when it came to gaining a market share over the competition. He viewed employee welfare, equality, and discrimination as annoyances and ignored them. The drivers and riders made up Uber's two-sided market. But he did not care about their safety and welfare.

Eventually, Kalanick's scandals impacted the business's bottom line, and the board forced him to resign as CEO. Three years after his resignation as CEO and eventual resignation from the Board of Directors, Uber still struggled to turn a profit. Kalanick's greed damaged the company's reputation, which will take a long time to recover.

THE ART OF GIVING
This style of leadership is easily recognizable. It is the dog-eat-dog mindset, where the leader sees the market as a zero-sum game; my win is the loss of my competitor, and their success

is my loss. This leader perceives the market as intensely competitive and will go to all lengths, perhaps even unethical or illegal means, to win that extra sale. In their mind, they are being smart and outwitting the competition (or public enforcement!) to win.

They fail to see that a rising tide lifts all boats. We are not better off by pulling someone else down. We are collectively better off when we help each other in the market.

Had Kalanick reacted by adopting initiatives to increase rider safety or improve drivers' earnings potential, Uber might have forced a sea change in the ride-hailing market—creating value not only for its riders and drivers but also for its competitors. And for his part, Kalanick might have been hailed as a Giver.

In his book, *Give and Take,* author Adam Grant characterizes Givers as contributors to others without expectation of a return. They are altruists. Based on Grant's research, leaders who are Givers are most likely to experience long-term success. [45]

In contrast, Takers have the "dog-eat-dog" mentality. Kalanick acted selfishly and for his interest, getting as much as he could from others. Takers tend to self-promote and take credit for group work instead of acknowledging the team's contribution. The disproportionate participation of Takers will eventually deplete the group's energy and motivation.

---

45   Adam Grant, *Give and Take: A Revolutionary Approach to Success.* Read by Brian Keith Lewis. Penguin Audio, 2013. Audible audio ed.

Leaders who recognize their responsibility and role in fixing wicked problems know that they don't operate in a zero-sum game. They know their actions and those of other players in the market are interdependent. They don't maximize to boost their profits; they maximize to lift all boats.

In the past, profit-maximizing capitalists perceived negotiation as a zero-sum game and taking as the art of the deal. Grant found negotiation no longer functions as a win-lose or zero-sum game. In his analysis of twenty-eight studies, Grant consistently found that the most successful negotiators cared as much about the other party's success as they did their own. We can't win until we create value. A successful negotiation is when everyone wins.[46]

We need a collaborative environment to create a profitable, purpose-driven business. This means building a team with Givers rather than Takers. Givers empower other team members because they have high empathy and build trusting relationships. Givers will also ensure that everyone achieves their purpose in the end.

IS THE BOSS ALWAYS RIGHT?

Sometimes in organizations, we see employees operating in silos with little collaboration. Each department jealously guards what they know. When we look at the leadership in these organizations, we will find a leader who thinks he has all the answers. No one in the company dares to challenge "the boss."

---

46   Adam Grant, "In Negotiations, Givers Are Smarter Than Takers," *The New York Times,* March 27, 2020.

Innovation and creativity, which we need to solve wicked problems, can't thrive in such environments.

Brené Brown, the author of *Dare to Lead*, would say this would not work.[47] When leaders drive for perfection and foster a fear of failure, they are practicing Armored Leadership. Such leaders associate their power and right to lead from their position in the organization or title.

You may recognize other characteristics of such leaders:
- They like being right.
- They use their power over others.
- They lead for control.
- They propagate a "fitting in" culture.
- They tolerate discrimination.

An organization led by Armored Leaders tends to shame and blame. Armored Leaders personally attack their employees rather than support them when they make a mistake. Corrosive relationships follow pain and anger.

By contrast, Brown advocates for Daring Leadership. Instead of having all the answers, Daring Leaders are learners. They cultivate a culture of belonging and inclusivity, welcoming diverse perspectives. These leaders genuinely appreciate feedback and want to see their blind spots. Leaders who merely pay lip service in asking for feedback alienate their team because they come across as unauthentic.

---

47 Brené Brown, *Dare to Lead: Brave Work. Tough Conversations. Whole Hearts.* Read by Brené Brown. Random House Audio, 2018. Audible audio ed.

Daring Leaders' organizations tend to have a high level of accountability. There is a vulnerability in sharing mistakes and learning the lesson together. The culture builds on rather than breaks relationships and stops collaboration. They don't shy away from difficult conversations that promote growth. Daring Leaders "lean into courage."[48]

Anita Roddick dared to do the opposite of what other capitalists were doing in 1976. She founded The Body Shop, using the business as a vehicle to change the world. She sourced products from exotic locations and ensured that the producers were paid fairly for them. Instead of exploiting developing nations and maximizing for profit, she decided to help them out of poverty.

She sought to lift all boats. She personally wrote newsletters to educate customers and employees about nature and the use of products.

Among the first global beauty brands to engage in cause marketing, The Body Shop advocated for an animal testing ban in the beauty industry. The brand's activism became its brand story, told through articles, interviews, and ads in glossy, fashion magazines. The story resonated with consumers. Customers were loyal to the brand because they felt bonded to a company that shared their values. Within twenty years, The Body Shop made $231 million in sales with little traditional marketing investment.[49]

---

48 "Dare to Lead," *Brené Brown*, accessed January 29, 2021.
49 "Anita Roddick," Entrepreneur, October 10, 2008

Roddick created a values-driven company in contrast to her peers, which focused on growth and more growth. She opened communication channels for feedback that enabled The Body Shop to deliver better products and services. Roddick was OK with not having all the answers and accepted making mistakes because this was how she could enrich her business as a leader.

CAN I BE A LEADER?

We looked at what constitutes good leadership in the context of creating profit and impact. But who is a leader?

Narrowly defined, a leader commands a group, organization, or country. But you don't need to have a title or be given the authority to be a leader. We follow people who step up and follow their purpose with courage. We follow those who do the right thing because they inspire us.

The more expansive definition of a leader is someone who has the qualities and characteristics we want to emulate. They don't mind being different and going against the grain, like Roddick, to pursue what is important. Instead of following the prescribed recipe of a leader, whether it is dressing a certain way or using particular business phrases, they speak authentically from their purpose. We follow such people because they bring others along with them to achieve a goal or cause.

Brown's definition of a leader requires a willingness to be vulnerable. She writes, "The courage to be vulnerable is not about winning or losing; it's about the courage to show up when you can't predict or control the outcome."[50]

No one needs to wait for permission to be a leader. Real leadership power comes from embodying inspirational behavior that springs others into action. Real power does not come from title, salary, or the number of people reporting to the person.

The story of Greta Thunberg reminds me of the quote, "Every small step in the right direction counts." When Thunberg was merely fifteen years old in August 2018, she started a protest against the Swedish Government for their lack of action on the climate crisis.[51] The world witnessed her relentless commitment as she camped outside the Swedish Parliament building, a lone figure holding up her plain white sign that read *School Strike for Climate.*

Under the umbrella name of Fridays for the Future, Thunberg started a movement. Her protest inspired other youth and students worldwide to step up and demand their governments keep the global temperature increase to below 1.5 degrees Celsius. The Fridays for the Future movement culminated when Thunberg appealed to political leaders at the United Nations Summit in 2019 to take action.[52] No one is too small or too young to make a difference.

---

50 Brené Brown, *Dare to Lead: Brave Work. Tough Conversations. Whole Hearts.* Read by Brené Brown. Random House Audio, 2018. Audible audio ed.

51 "Homepage," Fridays for the Future, accessed January 29, 2021.

52 Mahita Gajanan, "*You Have Stolen My Dreams and My Childhood:* Grete Thunberg Gives Powerful Speech at UN Climate Summit," *Time,* September 23, 2019.

The CEO or executive does not make decisions alone. Managers, employees, and customers can influence the direction of a business. Susan Fowler first spoke up against the sexism she experienced at Uber. She was not the company's first victim. Yet her courage and vulnerability made a difference in the work experience of other women in the company.

Dan O'Sullivan posted the first tweet that started the #DeleteUber campaign in response to what he saw as Uber taking advantage of a taxi drivers' strike in New York in January 2017 to gain market share.[53] This simple act had the power to cause Kalanick to defend Uber's actions to prevent further customer loss to his business.[54]

Each of us, no matter our station in the world—entrepreneur, CEO, team lead, or recent graduate—should see ourselves as individually and collectively responsible for the protection of the planet and people. The very act of making yourself accountable and starting to take action makes you a leader in your community.

Everyone has a part to play.

THE BOTTOM LINE

- The "growth above all else" mindset may result in short-term gains and profit. Ultimately, this behavior could end up hurting the company's reputation and profitability.

---

53 Zack Friedman, "Understand This Before You #DeleteUber," *Forbes*, February 1, 2017.

54 Travis Kalanick, "Standing up for What's Right," Facebook, January 28, 2017.

- Adam Grant, in his book *Give and Take*, defined Givers as contributors to others without expectation of a return. He described Givers as more likely to succeed in the long term and critical to building successful profitable purpose-driven businesses.
- Brené Brown, the author of *Dare to Lead*, recommends Daring Leadership to build organizations with a high level of accountability and collaboration.
- Each of us can be leaders by stepping up and inspiring others to take action. We each have a part to play in protecting the planet and taking care of our community.
- The following chapter highlights some of the alarm bells that indicate we need to evolve business leadership now, as any inaction would be costly for the planet, society, and business.

REFLECT

1. Name a few leaders with whom you have worked, who've made a positive impact or impression on you. How would you describe them?
2. What did they say or do to empower you?
3. Reflect on a less favorable leader you've encountered. How would you describe that leader?
4. What did they do to make the team less effective?
5. What could you improve yourself as a leader?

CHAPTER 4

WHY NOW?

More than 4.4 billion people use social media. Nearly two-thirds of the world's population spend around two-and-a-half hours scrolling through Facebook, Instagram, LinkedIn, YouTube, and Twitter every day.[55]

Private and public companies rely on social media platforms to push their latest news or communication directly to customers and to the public. Eighty percent of customers surveyed said they expect companies to respond to their social media posts within twenty-four hours. Half reported that they would cease business with a company that is non-responsive to negative posts.[56]

In the age of social media, a company's every action or inaction is transparent and visible for all to see. The company's digital footprints leave a permanent trail. Anyone can pull up

---

55 Ashley Viens, "This Graph Tells Us Who's Using Social Media the Most," *World Economic Forum,* October 2019.

56 Swetha Amaren, "What Are Your Customers' Expectations for Social Media Response Time?" *Hubspot*, accessed January 29, 2021.

historical posts and articles and see if the company's actions are consistent with their communication.

The public will repost or retweet when they perceive a company as inauthentic. They will not hesitate to make inconsistencies or greenwashing public.

For example, when a United Airlines flight attendant forcibly removed a passenger from an overbooked flight, another passenger in the cabin captured a video of the incident. That single passenger's tweeted video spread virally across all social networks. Many people criticized the airline's actions, and the company lost more than $500 million of value through a fall in its stock price.

Millennials use Twitter as their social media platform of choice.[57] They use Twitter to "cancel" or ostracize a person or brand in a modern-day form of boycotting online. Cancel culture publicly shames an individual or withdraws support from a business after an offensive act.

"This is the birth of Brand Democracy; as consumers are electing brands as their change agents," said Richard Edelman, CEO of the eponymous global marketing firm.[58]

Edelman found that, globally, a whopping 64 percent of consumers choose brands solely based on its values or stand on a political issue. A majority of 54 percent believed that it is

---

57 Katie Sehl, "Top Twitter Demographics That Matter to Social Media Marketers," *Hootsuite*, May 28, 2020.

58 "Two-Thirds of Consumers Worldwide Now Buy on Beliefs," Edelman, accessed January 29, 2021.

easier for the public to get brands to address social problems than to get the government to act.[59]

At the height of the Black Lives Matter movement, the public canceled CrossFit founder Greg Glassman in 2020 for a racist comment he posted on Twitter. The backlash for him and the fitness brand he founded was immediate.

Reebok severed its nine-year partnership with CrossFit. All-star athletes disassociated themselves from the company. Entrepreneurs and gyms operating franchises separated themselves from the brand.[60]

Cancel culture may not be the right solution to get business leaders to act differently. But we do know three things: social media gives the public a microphone to expose bad company behavior; cancel culture negatively impacts your bottom line; and leaders who fail to do things more intentionally risk being left behind.

FOLLOW THE MONEY

According to the Global Impact Investing Network, impact investments are "made ... to generate positive, measurable social and environmental impact alongside a financial return ... (C)apital (is provided) to address the world's most pressing challenges in sectors such as sustainable agriculture, renewable energy, conservation, microfinance, and

---

59 "Two-Thirds of Consumers Worldwide Now Buy on Beliefs," Edelman, accessed January 29, 2021.

60 Kyle Stock, "Sunday Strategist: CrossFit Isn't Canceled, But It's Close," *Bloomberg*, June 14, 2020.

affordable and accessible basic services, including housing, health care, and education."[61]

The nonprofit organization estimated 1720 organizations manage $715 billion of impact funds in 2020, compared to just $5 billion in 2013.[62] Immense wealth exploded into this area in just seven short years, growing over one hundred times. Investors range from family offices and individuals to traditional fund managers, financial institutions, and pension funds.

Similarly, Environmental, Social, and Governance (ESG) investing also exploded. In comparison with impact investing, ESG investors look at a company's behavior in:

- Energy use and conservation
- Vendor and labor relations
- Business practices such as conflicts of interest

Morningstar reported total investment in ESG funds had surpassed $1 trillion, with net inflows of $71 billion in the second quarter of 2020, driven by an interest in sustainable investing in the wake of the COVID-19 pandemic. ESG fund managers such as BlackRock carry a lot of weight in the market and could influence corporate executives to change how they lead their business. The pandemic "highlighted the importance of building sustainable and resilient business models based on multi-stakeholder considerations."[63]

---

61   "What You Need to Know About Impact Investing," *Global Impact Investing Network*, accessed January 29, 2021.

62   "What You Need to Know About Impact Investing," *Global Impact Investing Network*, accessed January 29, 2021.

63   Sam Meredith, "Sustainable Investment Funds Just Surpassed $1 Trillion for the First Time on Record," *CNBC*, August 11, 2020.

Wealth managers estimate millennials will hold five times as much wealth as they have today, inheriting more than $68 trillion from their Baby Boomer parents by 2030.[64] Millennials will inherit one of the most significant wealth transfers that will make this generation one of the wealthiest groups ever.

Currently, millennial millionaires make up about 2 percent of the total US population.[65] Baby Boomers far outnumber millennials, which will result in a wealth concentration in certain Millennial groups.

What does this mean for business?

We have started to witness how millennials will spend this wealth. One survey found that 87 percent of high-net-worth millennials will study a company's ESG track record before investing. Millennials want to grow their wealth in a way that is aligned with their values. This generation is more likely than baby boomers and Gen Xers to intentionally stop investing in a company because of the company's products or services' impact on the community.[66] This has caused a surge in interest in ESG funds and sustainability investing among this generation of investors.

Further, millennials would not hesitate to penalize businesses with values in conflict with their own, choosing to vote with

64 "A Look at Wealth 2019: Millennial Millionaires," *Coldwell Banker*, October 16, 2019.

65 Jack Kelly, "Millennials Will Become Richest Generation in American History as Baby Boomers Transfer Over Their Wealth," *Forbes*, October 26, 2019.

66 "Ethics and Investing: How Environmental, Social, and Governance Issues Impact Investor Behavior," Allianz.

their wallets and not work with such companies. Having grown up with the internet and smartphones, the first generation of digital natives often turns to social media when making purchase decisions.

Together with Gen Z, millennials continue to push the conversation of conscious consumerism in the marketplace.[67] Eighty-four percent of millennials expect the fashion industry in particular to have sustainable supply chains and eco-friendly products. More importantly, they proudly vote with their spending habits. Companies need to adapt their business practices or risk losing customers in the long run.

THE RIVER BETWEEN US
Fifty trillion dollars.

"That is how much the upward redistribution of income has cost American workers over the past several decades," proclaimed the *Time Magazine* report.[68] The report estimated the gap caused by the distribution of income between the super-rich and lower-wage families.

Fifty trillion dollars is almost 3.5 times the size of China's economy.[69]

---

67 Sally Ho, "Conscious Consumers: 10 Ways Millennials & Gen Zs Are Changing How & What We Buy," *Green* Queen, July 10, 2020.

68 Nick Hanauer, David Rolf, "The Top 1% of Americans Have Taken $50 Trillion From the Bottom 90%—And That's Made the U.S. Less Secure," *Time*, September 14, 2020.

69 The World Bank Database (accessed January 29, 2021).

The calculation was derived by looking at the cumulative inequality in the US between 1974 and 2018. Using the more equitable baseline income distribution from 1945 to 1974, the lower 90 percentile of Americans would have accumulated an aggregate income of $2.5 trillion more in 2018, and $47 trillion cumulative between 1975 and 2018.[70]

Real incomes grew close to the economic growth rate per capita across all income levels from 1947 to 1974, creating a prosperous middle class. However, since 1975, wealth did not grow at the same rate as the economy across income groups. The top 1 percent has, in fact, captured most of the economic growth of the US.[71]

Total taxable income of the top 1 percent grew from 9 percent in 1975 to 22 percent in 2018. In comparison, the bottom 90 percent experienced a decrease in income from 67 percent to 50 percent in the same period. So in effect, income transferred from most of the workers to the elite.[72]

The widening gap between the have and have nots is not just one of class and economic power. It is also one of race and gender. Those from wealthy families tend to hold better-paying jobs compared to minorities. More women work today compared to the 1970s, but they hold lower-paid positions, which gives rise to a gender pay gap.

---

70   Carter C. Price, Kathryn A. Edwards, "Trends in Income From 1975 to 2018," Rand Corporation, accessed January 29, 2021.
71   Nick Hanauer, David Rolf, "The Top 1% of Americans Have Taken $50 Trillion From the Bottom 90%—And That's Made the U.S. Less Secure," *Time*, September 14, 2020.
72   Ibid.

Why should the acceleration in inequality concern us?

Inequality in one generation leads to inequality in access and opportunity to the next. There is less social mobility than we may like to believe, despite diligence and effort. A lot still depends on the circumstances into which we were born and luck. Less social mobility leads to a rise in inequality.

Inheritance accounts for fewer cases of transmittance of wealth across generations than we think, merely 12 percent of cases studied. The more significant driver of wealth transmission from parent to child lies in investment in education. As much as 24 percent of the likelihood of a child gaining economic success later in life depends on the schools and universities they attend.[73]

Access to the right schools and universities depends on where one lives. Who our neighbors were and whether we grew up in an affluent neighborhood were factors beyond our control as children. Yet these factors influence which opportunities might be accessible to us later in life.

Our choice of partner further influences the success of our offspring. Assortative mating states we will probably marry someone of equal income or education.[74] This marriage of equals results in wealth and talent concentration in these two-high-income-earner families where parents give the best for their children. As like tends toward like, society becomes

73 "Rising Wealth Inequality: Causes, Consequences and Potential Responses," University of Michigan, accessed January 29, 2021.

74 Tyler Cowen, "The Marriages of Power Couples Reinforce Income Inequality," *New York Times*, December 14, 2015.

further separated as wealthy couples and families become less connected from their poorer neighbors. An us-versus-them mentality emerges.

The greater the income gap between neighborhoods, the more likely the rich neighbors fall victim to property crime.[75] Even more alarming is the correlation between inequality and violent crime.[76] While not the sole cause of violent crime, inequality contributes to instability and rising disquiet in society.

From an economic perspective, depressed incomes for the bottom 90 percent indicate a lost market opportunity for growth. Lower paying jobs lead to less disposable income to buy goods that drive the economy and fewer resources to build a more efficient market.

The ongoing Fourth Industrial Revolution (4IR), characterized by automation and digitization, further intensifies income inequality. Like previous industrial revolutions, many jobs will disappear. An estimated one-third of the workforce, those engaged in low-skilled and repetitive tasks, would be displaced.[77]

Of course, new jobs will be created through the 4IR. But as the COVID-19 pandemic accelerated digitalization and

75 Neil Metz and Maria Burdina, "How Neighborhood Inequality Leads to Higher Crime Rates," LSE, accessed January 29, 2021.

76 "The Stark Relationship between Income Inequality and Crime," *The Economist,* June 7, 2018.

77 James Manyika, Susan Lund, Michael Chui, Jacques Bughin, Jonathan Woetzel, Parul Batra, Ryan Ko, and Saurabh Sanghvi, "Jobs Lost, Jobs Gained: What the Future of Work Will Mean for Jobs, Skills, and Wages," *McKinsey & Company,* November 28, 2017.

pushed people to work from home, how quickly can those who have lost their jobs reskill and find new ones?

IT'S GETTING HOT IN HERE

"We are the first generation to feel the effect of climate change and **the last generation who can do something about it**," said Former US President Barack Obama.[78] Other leaders and scientists have echoed the need to take action.

Former UN Secretary-General Kofi Annan said, "The world is reaching the tipping point beyond which **climate change may become irreversible**. If this happens, we risk denying present and future generations the right to a healthy and sustainable planet—the whole of humanity stands to lose."[79]

Some experts believe there are already irreversible changes to the planet and we are in a state of emergency.

"One can see from space how the human race has changed the Earth. Nearly all of the available land has been cleared of forest and is now used for agriculture or urban development. The polar icecaps are shrinking, and the desert areas are increasing. At night, the Earth is no longer dark, but large areas are lit up. All of this is evidence that **human exploitation of the planet is reaching a critical limit**. But human demands and expectations are ever-increasing. We cannot continue to pollute the atmosphere, poison the ocean,

---

78 "Remarks by the President at UN Climate Change Summit," *Obama White House Archives,* September 23, 2014.

79 Nicola Davis, "Kofi Annan: We Must Challenge Climate-Change Sceptics Who Deny the Facts," *The Guardian,* May 3, 2015.

and exhaust the land. There isn't any more available," warned theoretical physicist Stephen Hawking.[80]

The rapid thaw and slow collapse of the West Antarctic ice sheet is a tipping point underway. The start of one tipping point could trigger another, in a domino chain-like effect. The Arctic melting and warming could trigger an increase in fires in North American forests, releasing more carbon into the atmosphere, adding to global warming. The intertwined systems of the planet mean that when one part of the house is on fire, it would be difficult to stop the spread to the rest of the house.

In 2015, 196 nations signed the Paris Agreement to limit the increase in global temperature to below two degrees Celsius, preferably 1.5 degrees Celsius. Scientists estimate that we will reach an increase of 1.5 degrees Celsius between 2030 and 2052 based on the current emissions rate.[81] We need to achieve net-zero emissions by 2050 to limit warming to 1.5 degrees Celsius.

Transportation, industry, and power sectors contribute more greenhouse gas emissions than other human activities. Achieving net-zero requires collective action by businesses and individuals, switching from fossil fuels to electrification, from private cars to public transit.

The impact of global warming by 1.5 degrees Celsius includes a reduction in crop yields, an interruption in

---

80   *The 11ᵗʰ Hour*, directed by Leila Conners and Nadia Conners (2009).
81   "Understanding Global Warming of 1.5°C," IPCC, accessed January 29, 2021.

water supply, and an increased spread of diseases. The effect will be unequally spread across geographies, with some of the poorer nations such as Haiti being hit harder. The results from climate change would further hamper their economic growth and increase the divide with developed countries.

THE OLD WAY CAN'T WORK

How we do business and approach wicked problems is not working. Incumbent leadership's focus on profits led to inequalities and the devastation of our environment. We need a new mindset for a more stable and sustainable world for future generations.

Because of the proliferation of social media, the growth in impact funds, and the needs of millennials and Gen Z, businesses and their leaders need to be more values driven. If they are not already creating a positive impact through business, they need to start now.

The income inequality that will soon be made worse by the Fourth Industrial Revolution and global warming indicates that society and the planet are on the precipice of disaster. Those who hold the reins to capital are in part the cause and have the power to remedy the unstable situation now.

In the old dog-eat-dog world, business was thought of as a series of transactions. In this new order, we need to be in the business of relationships. Instead of what can I get out of this person or transaction, ask what can we do together to create a more positive impact?

Instead of thinking short term on a transaction-by-transaction basis, ask how your action here affects the other stakeholders further down the line and in the long term? If you choose to use more expensive recycled material, don't just think about the additional cost burden. Ask as well how the benefits are multiplied.

THE BOTTOM LINE

- In **Part I** of this book, we looked at leadership behaviors that came from profit maximization. Social and environmental issues were left to public and nonprofit organizations to solve.

- This chapter made clear that business leaders need to evolve their mindset now. First, the proliferation of technology and social media has increased the spotlight and transparency on business activities. Some have taken to social media to boycott businesses, which results in a negative financial impact.

- Investors' interests have started to shift as indicated by the explosion in money poured into sustainability funds in 2020. Increasingly, millennials and Gen Z vote with their wallets and choose to buy only from companies that match their values.

- Income inequality correlated with class, race, and gender inequality, has reached a level that harms society. The ongoing Fourth Industrial Revolution will further increase the gap, as it negatively impacts those with less capital while benefiting the top 1 percent.

- Global warming has reached a state of emergency where irreversible changes have occurred. We need to take collective action to prevent further irreparable damage.

- In **Part II**, we dive into **The Altruistic Capitalist** mindset. The following chapter introduces mindfulness as one of the foundations to build a purpose-driven business.

REFLECT

1. Recall a recent example of cancel culture. How could the company have improved communication and resolved the situation?
2. How do your values influence your buying or investing decisions?
3. How can business decrease inequality? Discuss with specific examples.

PART II

THE ALTRUISTIC CAPITALIST MINDSET

The most precious gift we can offer anyone is our attention.

THICH NHAT HANH

CHAPTER 5

THE MINDSET OF THE MONK: MINDFULNESS

———

When comedian Roseanne Barr tweeted a short forty-four-character racist insult, it took only five minutes for her boss to decide how to handle it. It was 2018, and The Walt Disney Company—with CEO Robert Iger at the helm—had rebooted Barr's eponymous series with much success. With her new show riding high in the ratings, Barr went low, publicly referring to a former Obama administration advisor as an ape.

Firing Barr meant the cancellation of the sitcom and, in turn, the loss of millions of dollars in revenue for Disney.

"I didn't think of any financial repercussion despite *Roseanne* being the biggest show on TV ... We have to do what's right. Not what's politically correct, and not what's commercially correct. Just what's right," Iger explained.[82]

---

82 Robert Iger, *The Ride of a Lifetime: Lessons Learned from 15 Years as CEO of the Walt Disney Company.* Read by Jim Frangione and Robert Iger. Random House Audio, 2019. Audible audio ed.

The clarity Iger had in making this decision intrigued me. It was not the first time he had taken a commercial risk as CEO of the global media and entertainment conglomerate.

In June 2016, an alligator dragged a two-year-old boy into the lagoon at a Disney resort in Florida. Many senior executives, including Iger, were in Shanghai to launch a new park that the team had been working on for seventeen years.

Amid launch preparations and meeting with Chinese officials, Iger called the boy's family and offered his condolences. His decision to call the parents was risky. The call could have implicated the culpability of the company.[83]

But Iger did what he believed was humane. He was deeply empathetic, promising the boy's father that such a tragedy would not happen again to another child on Disney's property. Within twenty-four hours of the call, Iger's team installed warning signs and other security measures across the resort property. Similar to how he managed the Roseanne Barr situation, Iger acted with swiftness and certainty.

How does Iger achieve such clarity in thought and certainty in his actions?

He starts his daily routine in solitude. He wakes up around 4:15 a.m. and spends the next hour or so working out. The room is darkened, and he may turn on some music. But he mostly ignores the music. The most important aspect of his routine is not looking at his phone until after his workout.

---

83   Ibid.

This time alone enables him to focus, which increases Iger's creativity and effectiveness throughout the day.[84]

Leaders like Iger often face situations where they need to decide between maximizing profit and staying true to the team's purpose. There is no obvious right choice; choosing profit could come at the cost of sacrificing the business's commitment to fairness and equality. Different stakeholders may complicate the decision-making process by demanding that business leaders should prioritize their needs over others. The one who wins is sometimes the one with the loudest voice or who shouts the longest.

Yuval Harari, the author of *Sapiens*, practices Vipassana meditation to help him cut out the noise and clutter.

"When you train the mind to focus on something like the breath, it also gives you the discipline to focus on much bigger things and to really tell the difference between what's important and everything else … The discipline to have this focus I really got from the meditation."[85]

Instead of meditation, Iger uses his morning workouts to get clarity and focus on the things that matter. This helps him make decisions when there are no clear answers. He makes his decisions based on his core values of integrity and fairness.[86] Barr's racist post went against the high ethical

---

84 Hao, "Bob Iger: Daily Routine," *Balance the Grind,* August 16, 2020.

85 Ezra Klein, "Yuval Harari, Author of *Sapiens*, on How Meditation Made Him a Better Historian," *Vox*, February 28, 2017.

86 Robert Iger, *The Ride of a Lifetime: Lessons Learned from 15 Years as CEO of The Walt Disney Company.* Read by Jim Frangione and Robert Iger. Random House Audio, 2019. Audible audio ed.

standards Iger set for himself and his team. Even though firing Barr could have jeopardized his network business's ratings and sales, Iger prioritized maintaining the business's integrity.

When Iger had to respond to the Florida tragedy, he focused on fairness. He empathized with the child's parents and risked potential legal liability. Ultimately, his decision confirmed the public's trust in Disney to prioritize their customers' safety, protecting the brand in the long run.

Under Iger's fifteen-year leadership as CEO, Disney's net income went from $2.5 billion in 2005 to $10.4 billion in 2019.[87] Iger revitalized the once-tired brand through four large and strategic acquisitions of Pixar Animation Studios, Marvel Entertainment, Lucasfilm, and 20th Century Fox. As Jiminy Cricket said to Pinocchio, in a 1940 Disney animated movie, "Always let your conscience be your guide." Iger's business acumen and conscience led to financial growth and increased brand equity.

SELF-REFLECTION AND HUMILITY

How do you step down as managing director of a company you founded?

Steve Schmida, the founder of Resonance Global, had to make that decision fifteen years after bootstrapping the advisory firm from his home's spare bedroom. As a business grows into the different phases, an entrepreneur may experience founder's dilemma.

---

87   SEC company filings.

Schmida was responsible for client and partner relationships and also decided on operations, including employee and accounting issues. As the business grew, he struggled to keep up with demands for his time. This caused delays in decision-making and confusion in the office. He was exhausted and frustrated, and there was growing tension within the senior leadership team. If he didn't deal with the situation quickly, his inability to manage his time could negatively impact his client relationships in the public and private sector and internal team relations.

Schmida told me it took him up to eighteen months to step into a different role at the firm. It was one of the hardest decisions he had to make. He built on his self-awareness, both from an intellectual and an emotional perspective.

"I had to be self-aware enough to realize that it had come to the time when it was better for someone else to lead the company. I was holding it back ... I don't have the right aptitude to give the company the structure that it needs."

From an emotional perspective, he said, "Ego ... is a huge factor. When I started the company, people thought I was crazy. I had a point to prove ... When things started to gain momentum ... (ego got in the way of having) a clear judgment."

Resonance develops sustainable solutions for public- and private-sector clients in areas such as food security and global health. Organizations and individuals alike should develop an awareness of their strengths and weaknesses to perform at their highest potential. When we have humility and accept our limits, we can reduce frustration and move forward quickly to overcome challenges.

No single person, team, or company can solve the problems that plague the planet or society. We can only be part of the bigger ecosystem that solves the problem together. Set aside egos and build alliances and partnerships. The focus should not be on how much attention and credit you can get but on how much impact you can create in working together with others.

Doing what is right matters more than insisting on *being* right or *being seen to be* right.

Turning over the managing director reins to the business's cofounder turned out to be the best decision for both him and the firm. Schmida reflected on his interests, passion, and what he brought to the table: the vision and creativity to arrive at this decision. He also let go of his ego and attachment to being in charge.

The business could flourish again. In his new role as chief innovation officer, Schmida brings more coherence to the vision and drives the thought leadership needed to support the business's clients to create a positive impact in emerging markets.

FROM BEING PRESENT TO EMPATHY

In both the examples of Iger and Schmida, we observed how the practice of reflection-solitude and mindfulness-empowered them to make better decisions for their business.

Satya Nadella, the CEO of Microsoft, starts his morning with a daily ritual. "The first thing I do when I get up in the morning … (is to) put (my) feet down and say what (I'm) thankful for and what (I'm) looking forward to."[88]

This short and simple mindfulness ritual brings Nadella's focus on feelings of gratitude in the present moment. We feel less overwhelmed and more optimistic when we are grateful. When we notice the joyful things in our life, we also see growth opportunities. The regular practice of gratitude improves mental well-being in the long run.

This daily ritual and a family misfortune at the age of twenty-nine helped shape Nadella into the mindful leader he is today.

Nadella had recently completed his MBA at The University of Chicago Booth School of Business. He and his wife, Anu, were expecting their first child. As an architect, she planned on returning to work after their child was born. Both were settling into their new life together in Seattle, having left their families far away in India. They spent months preparing for their first child's arrival—decorating the nursery and buying the necessary items to welcome the baby.

They could not have predicted how their lives were about to change. Zain, their first child, suffered from in-utero asphyxiation and cerebral palsy, which rendered him a person with quadriplegia. It was not the carefree life that Nadella or his young bride imagined, but one filled with doctors, therapists, and surgeries.

---

88 Jessica Stillman, "This 5-Second Morning Ritual Sets Satya Nadella Up for All-Day Success," *Inc.*, June 17, 2020.

Devastated, Nadella questioned, "How could this be happening to me?"[89]

After his wife recovered from the emergency cesarean, she immediately went into action and took up the charge of learning what could be done for their son and how they could best take care of him.

It would take Nadella a few years to see the situation differently. Nothing had happened to him; something had happened to his son. He started to look at what he could do to improve his son's life.

Through Nadella's reflection, he developed a deep sense of empathy. It became the source of all his actions, and when he became the CEO of Microsoft in 2014, he made empathy a part of his leadership and transformed the company's culture.

Microsoft was fraught with internal competition when Nadella was appointed CEO. The internal battles were so known that Manu Cornet, a cartoonist, had illustrated the company's organizational structure as warring factions. "Innovation was being replaced by bureaucracy. Teamwork was being replaced by internal politics. We were falling behind,"[90] described Nadella of that period.

Empathy follows from the practice of mindfulness and reflection. When we are more empathetic, we become better

---

89 Satya Nadella, *Hit Refresh: The Quest to Rediscover Microsoft's Soul and Imagine a Better Future for Everyone*. Read by Shridhar Solanki and Satya Nadella. Harper Audio, 2017, Audible audio ed.

90 Ibid.

listeners. We feel a deeper connection to those around us when we listen more authentically and feel our voices are heard. This, in turn, increases collaboration within teams and builds the trust needed for collective action to solve social causes and environmental damage.

In the course of being more self-aware, Nadella learned to forgive himself. He learned humility. "None of us is perfect; none of us will be perfect. Once you come to that deeper realization, you don't judge as quickly, you listen better, and you can amplify people's strengths versus focusing on their weaknesses. I think my road to empathy has been possible because of my ability to confront my own mistakes and shortcomings."[91]

In just six years under Nadella's leadership, Microsoft transformed culturally and strategically. Operating income grew from $28 billion in 2014 to $53 billion in 2020. Nadella changed practices inside and outside the company—he introduced initiatives that encouraged more collaboration across Microsoft departments and developed partnerships with other tech players in the market.

FROM MINDFULNESS TO PURPOSE

Mindfulness is about relaxing. Mindfulness is about having no thoughts. Mindfulness is about being isolated. Mindfulness is only for introverts and the self-absorbed. Mindfulness weakens your perseverance. Mindfulness makes you apathetic.

---

91   Amit Chowdhry, "Microsoft Monday: Satya Nadella's *'Hit Refresh,'* Office 2019, Microsoft Windows Store Gets Rebranded," *Forbes*, October 2, 2017.

These are all myths.

Mindfulness is the practice of being in the present and being aware of your thoughts, feelings, and sensations without judgment, from moment to moment. You can train to be more mindful through meditation.

Although one of the ancillary benefits of mindfulness is reduced anxiety and depression, the goal of meditation is not to relax. During meditation, theta waves become the most dominant waves in our brain. Theta waves encourage creativity, improve problem-solving skills and memory, and sharpen focus.[92]

"I can't meditate; my mind is too active and I have too many thoughts" is a common excuse for not meditating. It is not true that you need to have no thoughts to meditate. Instead, during meditation, you observe your thoughts as they occur and choose not to react to them.

Extroverts may disavow meditation because it is only for the "quiet folks." While it is true that meditation often takes place in solitude, increased mindfulness actually deepens your connection with others around you. Nadella's mindfulness practice increased his empathy and compassion; he learned to build stronger relationships. Rather than isolating individuals, teams that meditate together experience more solidarity and social connection.

---

92 "Brainwaves the Language," Neurohealth, accessed January 25, 2021.

Meditation is not for the weak and does not weaken you. In fact, being more mindful strengthens resolve and grows grit. Being able to stand apart from your feelings, observe the bare facts, be less impulsive, and maintain focus on priorities enables meditators to better achieve their goals.

Being mindful is about accepting the present without judgment. In no way does acceptance mean apathy or being morally ambivalent. The opposite is more likely to be true. Because mindfulness leads to increased empathy, compassion, and improved problem-solving skills, meditators are also likely to be more caring. Most of the social entrepreneurs I interviewed practice some form of mindfulness.

Jack Dorsey, CEO of Twitter and Square, also practices Vipassana meditation. "Meditation is about honing your skills of observation and making sure that we are present and aware of everything that we are doing and that we are not just blindly reacting to it ... we're fully aware of the what and also the why and able to make choices around it."[93]

Sophie Bachmann, founder of Zen & Go, a consultancy that trains executives on mindfulness, agreed that we could learn to expand the space between stimulus and response through regular mindfulness practice.

She quoted Viktor Frankl in *Man's Search for Meaning*, "Between stimulus and response, there is a space. In that

---

93   Richie Crowley, "Jack Dorsey on Mindfulness in Under 2 Minutes," *Medium* (blog), May 28, 2020.

space is our power to choose our response. In our response lies our growth and our freedom."[94]

When we are more mindful, we minimize the risk of making poor decisions that may be clouded by feelings, illusions, and assumptions.

After investing time in self-reflection, Schmida came up with a solution that brought more value to the firm. He set aside feelings of pride and the need to be part of every decision made. All stakeholders, including himself, came out winning in the end.

Bachmann shared with me her experience of leading mindfulness workshops with corporate executives. During her eight-week program, she teaches executives resilience, mindful communication, and mindfulness tools. Course participants reported an increase of between 12–19 percent in creativity, focus, and well-being. Ultimately, this leads to increased productivity at work.

Mindfulness is good for the self and business.

THE BOTTOM LINE
- Robert Iger, CEO of The Walt Disney Company, could make decisions when there were no obvious answers because he had a clarity of purpose. He achieves this clarity through incorporating reflection and solitude into his day.

---

94 Viktor Frankl, *Man's Search for Meaning* (Boston: Beacon Press, 2006).

- Steve Schmida, founder of Resonance Global, increased his self-awareness and humility, which led to business growth. He learned to let go of his ego that caused bottlenecks in the business.
- Satya Nadella, CEO of Microsoft, starts his morning with a gratitude exercise. A personal tragedy developed empathy in Nadella. He transformed the culture at Microsoft to include empathy, which led to new innovations and financial growth.
- The benefits of mindfulness include increased creativity, focus, and reduced reactivity to emotional triggers.
- We look at how some companies have included mindfulness in their culture in Chapter 6.

REFLECT

1. What core values do you believe in and which drive you? What behaviors support these values?
2. Which parts of your work are aligned with your core values?
3. How does your ego limit you at work?
4. What are the core values of your stakeholders (employees, customers, suppliers, and investors)?
5. Do your core values align with that of your stakeholders?

CHAPTER 6

INSIDE THE MINDSET OF A MONK

———

Ding.

Everyone in the room settled into their seats. Silence fell across the room. There was no shuffling of notes, and no one looked at their phones. Some looked down; some closed their eyes.

After a full minute, the meeting started.

All meetings at Eileen Fisher, Inc., a women's fashion company, start this way. Its products are synonymous with simplicity and sustainability.[95] The business champions leadership programs for women and girls and provides grants to improve women's representation in creating positive environmental outcomes.[96]

---

95 "Company Overview," Eileen Fisher, Inc., accessed January 24, 2021.
96 "Environmental Justice Grant," Eileen Fisher, Inc., accessed January 24, 2021.

"The moment of silence we take before meetings at the company ... [allows me] to stop and just notice what's ... presenting itself in front of me," explained Eileen Fisher, the founder of the company.

Around the table, Fisher and her team spent sixty full seconds in quiet contemplation, each person in their thoughts. With each passing breath, the mood seemed to lift, and even the room seemed brighter. When the full minute was up, everyone shared how they felt and what they would like to achieve for that day.

Business executives often find themselves rushing from one meeting to the next without a moment's pause. They arrive breathless and a few minutes late to the room from another meeting. They scramble to gather their thoughts and get up to speed with the discussion that has started. At the end of another long day of back-to-back meetings, the busy executive then finally sits down to do "actual work," firing off emails and attending to decisions to put out the fires in the organization.

No wonder so many of us feel overwhelmed, a familiar knot forming in our neck or upper back. In high-performance cultures with the pressure of getting more and more done, it seems counter-intuitive to slow down. Pause. Stop.

At Eileen Fisher, the pause at the start of each meeting gives team members a chance to check-in. Where are you coming from? What are you dealing with today? Each of us has professional and personal priorities to juggle. Notably, we have fewer visual cues and opportunities to know what our team members are dealing with in a work-from-home environment.

The short practice of asking sincerely "How are you today?" before you start can make a big difference on the other people in the meeting. It makes others feel that they are heard, appreciated, and respected.

Good business practice tells us to start meetings with the objective and agenda for the day. An even better practice is to give everyone space to reset and share what they are going through, and then going into the objective and agenda. The simple five-minute exercise acts as a reset and brings everyone to the same mind space.

Fisher roots her mindful leadership in active listening. She does this by intentionally and vulnerably declaring, "I don't know."

Although the company designs and produces clothes, Fisher did not know anything about the business when she started it, having graduated from interior design at the University of Illinois. So she had to rely on others to help her produce her initial designs and products. She learned to listen to others intently.

"I've always been a 'don't knower,'" she claimed, her big soft eyes peering out from behind dark-rimmed glasses.[97] In her experience, being vulnerable with others about what she did not know led to others opening up to her. They wanted to help her and share their knowledge and experience.

As a leader in her company, this approach empowered her team. Employees stepped up. Instead of waiting for Fisher

---

97 Matt Tenney, "Be a 'Don't Knower': One of Eileen Fisher's Secrets to Success," *Huffington Post*, May 15, 2015.

to direct them on what to do, they felt safe to explore ideas and be accountable for the business themselves. It gave the team a sense of ownership.

This led to a less hierarchical and more collaborative approach to solving problems. Ultimately, this led to a more resilient team structure that is less dependent on any individual to make decisions.

It is incredible to imagine that a woman who did not know anything about making clothing is behind the twelve-hundred-employee clothing company. The company is less than four decades old and valued at $400 million.[98] Employees are proud to work at the company, and customers are loyal because of the brand promise of sustainability and inclusion.

THE TOUCHY-FEELY MYTH

The first word that comes to some people's minds when they hear mindfulness is touchy-feely. Mindfulness does not seem grounded in science. Meditation may appear overly spiritual or religious for others, so they reject mindfulness as well. Neither of these two misconceptions is true.

In my review of available literature and research, I found mindfulness reduces stress and mitigates burnout from the perpetual state of being online with our digital devices. Mindfulness also increases productivity at work because regular practice leads to enhanced focus and higher engagement

---

98   Haley Draznin, "Eileen Fisher Built a Fashion Empire. Her Employees Now Own Nearly Half of It," *CNN Business*, January 6, 2020.

on tasks. Another study found that a mere few minutes of mindfulness could improve brainstorming sessions.[99] It is no wonder increasingly more companies offer meditation as a benefit to their employees, including Google.

Chade-Meng Tan "hopes to see every workplace in the world become a drinking fountain of happiness and enlightenment."[100] As Employee No. 107 at Google, he was every bit of what you'd expect from an overachieving software engineer at one of the largest tech companies in the world.

By the time he was twelve, he had taught himself to code. At fifteen, he won his first national academic award. By seventeen, he was part of the national software championship team in his home country of Singapore.[101]

After completing a degree in computer science, he was offered a job at Google within five minutes of submitting his application.[102] By many accounts, he would be considered successful and therefore happy.

Except that he wasn't. His coworkers were also unhappy and stressed. In the race to achieve more and to do more, they found themselves wanting. So Tan set out to find a solution for a stress-free life for himself and his coworkers.

---

99   Nate Klemp, "5 Reasons Your Company Should Be Investing in Mindfulness Training," *Inc.*, October 17, 2019.
100 "About Meng," Chade-Meng Tan, accessed January 24, 2021.
101 Caitlin Kelly, "OK, Google, Take a Deep Breath," *New York Times*, April 28, 2012.
102 Ibid.

His search led him to mindfulness. Tan found that mindfulness encompassed not only meditation but also moments of reflection throughout the day. His initial efforts to launch meditation courses at Google failed. The word itself, "meditation," was not attractive to engineers who were drawn to facts. They thought meditation was fluffy and lacked serious substance.

But Tan knew from his experience that mindfulness helped him feel tangibly better. He wanted to share his results with his coworkers and help them feel happier too. So he positioned the course as an emotional intelligence and well-being course. This was the birth of Search Inside Yourself (SIY).

He divided the program into three parts his coworkers could easily apply in their daily work:
- Attention training
- Self-knowledge, which translates into the ability to control your emotions
- Mental habits[103]

Under attention training, Tan encouraged his coworkers to avoid reacting to emails but to step away and pause first. In his haste to clear out his inbox, Tan found that he had failed to consider the impact of his words and tones on the email's recipient. We often find it easy to push out messages in our inbox without being more thoughtful in our response, not knowing if our words could hurt or damage the relationship.

---

103 Drake Baer, "Here's What Google Teachers Employees in Its *Search Inside Yourself* Course," *Business Insider*, August 5, 2014.

Tan taught his coworkers to practice kindness under mental habits. He reasoned that when we help others or give to charity, we feel lighter and happier. So when his coworkers practice sending positive thoughts or wishing difficult coworkers well, relationships within the organization could improve.

Gratitude, as we saw in Chapter 5, springs from mindfulness. Tan also advocated logging moments of joy.[104] We are more likely to conclude that a day was a good one when we acknowledge and even proclaim those moments loudly during the day when we are happy. Robert Emmons, a professor of psychology, found that practicing gratitude for two weeks lowered perceived stress by 28 percent and depression by 16 percent, among other benefits.[105]

Focusing on gratitude reduces the feeling of being overwhelmed and enables us to see growth opportunities. This easy and powerful ritual shifts your perspective throughout the day subconsciously.

Honoring mini victories in projects, no matter how small, can motivate our teams to progress in their work. When we show others how their work contributes to projects, they become more engaged because they see their work as meaningful.

Tan positioned the mindfulness course as a practical training program where participants could be more productive and successful through being better people. He taught simple

---

104 David G Allan, "The Google Engineer Teaching Happiness in Three Steps," *BBC Future*, November 10, 2014.

105 "Gratitude Is Good Medicine," UC Davis Health Medical Center, November 25, 2015.

and easy techniques that participants could adopt in their daily workday.

The course gained strong traction within the skeptical class of engineers and scientists at Google because of the practical nature of the techniques and direct and secular language Tan used. The course gave participants a tool kit to navigate themselves and their teams through the uncertainty and pressure of working in the high-stakes field of technology.

Tan understood his audience and tailored the program content and language to suit its culture and values. He confronted misperceptions about mindfulness early on and invested time in researching the science behind it.

MEDITATION IN THE CULTURE

If we know mindfulness can help build a culture of using business as a force for good, how do we bring the whole organization on board?

According to Eivind Slaaen, head of people and culture development at Hilti—a supplier for the construction industry—senior executives need to be responsible for their organization's culture. As Albert Schweitzer, the Nobel Peace Prize winner said, "Example is not the main thing in influencing others. It is the only thing."

Putting accountability into executives' hands ensures that leaders embed culture in the organization as an item on top of their agenda, rather than something pushed out by the human resources team. Slaaen regularly examines the organization's culture with the executive team to design their development programs, which they name Culture Journey with Team Camps.

Recent changes in the industry caused stress at Hilti. The future looked uncertain. The executive team wanted to build resilience and help their employees overcome external market challenges. They also realized the need to support their employees in dealing with personal life issues, which may impact their work performance. For example, feeling overwhelmed at home may influence an employee's perception of workload, causing stress. With these objectives in mind, Slaaen put mindfulness at the heart of their latest Team Camp.

This Team Camp focused on increasing mental health so that their team could perform at their best level. Slaaen found that when the company showed they cared for their employees, teams were more engaged and motivated at work. The training shifted the tone within the office as managers and peers paid more attention to one another. Relationships improved.

I asked Slaaen how the company implements the program consistently for thirty thousand employees located across different office locations in the world.

Seventy internal trainers and coaches, called Sherpas, facilitate the two-day Team Camp programs around the world throughout the year, he explained. More importantly, the executive board trains their direct reports.

Managers run through the training twice, first as participants and second as leaders with their teams. In the second round, the Sherpa facilitates the full session while the manager plays a pivotal role in providing direction and support to their team.

Even the board of directors, which is external to the company, receives the Team Camp training. This helps reinforce the mindset of mindfulness throughout the organization. Learners internalize and remember lessons best when they teach others.

In addition, employees can customize their training. Each person is responsible for their own learning and development. Slaaen explained that personal accountability helps behavior change stick. The other ingredients for successful behavior change are tools to track their progress and community.

Two tools that Slaaen and his team developed are a mindfulness app and a heart rate tracker. The app provides guided meditations to supplement Team Camp trainings and help employees manage stress during the day. Both tools help employees review their progress and monitor their physical and mental health. During COVID-19, Sherpas facilitated resilience workshops and provided remote working guides that helped teams navigate the additional stress during the pandemic.

Community, specifically the language employees learned during Team Camp, helped the behavior change stick. The common language used among participants helps with accountability in the Team Camp community. For instance, if Person A goes off track during a meeting, Person B may remind Person A of the active listening exercise at Team

Camp. During the active listening exercise, one person practices listening attentively. But in the second round, the same person intentionally appears distracted, playing with his phone and looking around. When Person B mentions this exercise at the meeting, they bring Person A back to the present and focus their attention again on the topic at hand.

Sherpas and managers regularly check in on their respective communities to support their teams with their mindfulness practice. These in-built processes in the training help reinforce the learning and culture of mindfulness throughout the organization.

THE BOTTOM LINE

- At Eileen Fisher, Inc., the simple practice of beginning meetings with a pause enables team members to actively listen to each other. Eileen Fisher, the founder, also intentionally declares "I don't know" to empower her team to step up and share ideas.
- Chade-Meng Tan successfully established a mindfulness program at Google by teaching practical and easy exercises that participants could incorporate into their day. Exercises included logging in moments of joy and wishing others well. He intentionally used technical language and positioned the course as an emotional intelligence course that increased traction in the program.
- Eivind Slaaen scaled the mindfulness program at Hilti by enrolling managers to support their teams' training. Slaaen also gave team members accountability for their own learning and equipped them with tools to support their own learning. Another important aspect was the

community built during training that helped assimilation at the workplace.

- The following chapter introduces curiosity and presents the form it takes at work.

REFLECT

1. What areas of your work could benefit from slowing down?
2. What may stand in the way of your mindfulness practice?
3. Identify examples of how you could be more mindful.
4. Recall a recent milestone. Set aside some time to reflect on it.
5. How could you show your appreciation at work today?

CHAPTER 7

THE MINDSET OF THE FIVE-YEAR-OLD: CURIOSITY

———

"Why do I have to go to school?"
"Why do I have to eat vegetables?"
"Where do babies come from?"

If you've spent any time with a five-year-old, you recognize the bombardment of questions. They are curious, turning over every rock and taking apart toys in their quest for knowledge.

They don't want to annoy you. They don't even necessarily want your attention. They just want to discover the world around them.

Learning is a pleasurable experience that comes from the anticipated joy of finding the answer. In anticipation of the reward (the answer), our brains release dopamine, a chemical that regulates pleasure and reward.

When we are in this state of curiosity, the hippocampus, which regulates our learning and memory, becomes activated. The more activity we experience in this area, the better we remember. [106] Think back to a moment of intense anticipation, such as an announcement you'd been waiting for. You'd remember the moment clearly.

When we seek novelty in life and find wonder in the world, we retain our youthfulness and have better mental well-being. When we ask questions and show genuine interest in others, we develop close relationships based on trust. [107]

Somewhere along the way, some of us lose our eagerness to learn. [108] We might invest less in our learning because we think we are "smarter." We might become anxious with uncertainty and uncomfortable with our ignorance.

As business leaders, we're sometimes afraid of looking incompetent or indecisive when we ask questions. [109] In this case, asking questions does not lead to the anticipation of a reward.

---

106 Matthias J. Gruber and Charan Ranganath, "How Curiosity Enhances Hippocampus-Dependent Memory: The Prediction, Appraisal, Curiosity, and Exploration (PACE) Framework," *Trends in Cognitive Sciences*, November 6, 2019.

107 Amy Gallo, "How to Build the Social Ties You Need at Work," *Harvard Business Review*, September 23, 2015.

108 Mary Whatley, "The Benefits of Maintaining a Curious Mind in Older Age," *Psychology in Action*, February 20, 2020.

109 Natalia Karelaia, "When in Doubt, Leaders Should Ask Questions," *INSEAD*. March 9, 2020.

Instead, we anticipate others may judge us as unintelligent. Fear may be lingering in the background. There is no dopamine hit.

Other times, we are overly confident of our knowledge or experience and don't stop to probe further. For instance, when we interview for new hires, we use our experience with previous candidates to decide on the present ones. In adopting past conclusions, we may unfairly and incorrectly judge a candidate based on how they are dressed or what school they graduated from. Our subconscious decided before we learn more about this candidate.

This is an example of cognitive schema, when we use our past experience to guide our future actions and make sense of the present. By taking shortcuts to interpret the vast amount of data in our environment, our brain conserves energy and becomes more efficient.[110]

We use cognitive schema at work through team structure and processes. We capture data and build collective knowledge to avoid making the same mistake twice. This saves time and effort.

In this quest for efficiency, though, we may be prone to lose sight of our curiosity. Schemas can contribute to stereotypes and confirm pre-existing beliefs and ideas.[111] We may stop asking questions. We may reject information that does not fit with our established ideas and make the wrong choices. Taken

110 Kendra Cherry, "The Role of a Schema in Psychology," *Very Well Mind*, September 23, 2019.

111 John R. Anderson, *Cognitive Psychology and Its Implications* (New York: Worth Publishers, 2010), 153.

to the extreme, we are less resilient in times of uncertainty when the information does not fit our existing schema.

A company working to create a positive impact and profit is often enmeshed in uncertainty. We can't always do things the tried-and-tested way. If a company was founded decades ago, chances are it may need to update some of its supply chain practices and disrupt processes. How does it balance the interests of vendors and shareholders during the transformation? How does it manage the anxiety of employees during a reorganization? The risk of overly lean operations is less resilience and little room to maneuver when the course is not clear.

WHY NOT?

Dr. William Campbell was experimenting with Ivermectin in his research lab at Merck in 1978. Ivermectin, an antiparasitic for cattle, was one of four blockbuster drugs sold by Merck. He found that Ivermectin was effective against a gastrointestinal parasite found in horses. This parasite was similar to a human parasite that caused river blindness.[112]

He wondered if the animal health product could be used on humans.[113]

This line of questioning is common at Merck. The pharmaceutical company encourages Dr. Campbell and other scientists to follow new leads and be creative.

---

112 W. Michael Hoffman, Robert E. Frederick, Mark S. Schwartz, "Business Ethics: Readings and Cases in Corporate Morality" (5th ed), John Wiley & Sons, Inc. (2014).

113 Ibid.

Dr. Campbell was interested in whether Ivermectin could be used to help victims of river blindness who lived near rivers in the tropical regions of Africa and Latin America. The disease, labeled by the World Health Organization (WHO) as a public health and socioeconomic problem, caused great suffering for communities in thirty-five developing countries.

The rivers provide a breeding ground for the black flies that spread the disease. The biting fly passes along a parasitic worm. The worm moves through the bite wound to grow inside the human body. The body's immune response to the parasite causes severe itching and skin lesions. Extreme cases of the disease result in blindness. In the most extreme cases, the itch can become so severe that patients commit suicide.[114]

Doctors first identified the disease in 1893, but nearly one hundred years later, they still had no safe and effective treatment for patients. The disease afflicted inhabitants of rural river regions who tended to be poor. So river blindness disproportionately afflicted rural and poor populations who could not afford to pay for expensive medication. This made river blindness unattractive to pharmaceutical companies because they couldn't price the treatments high enough to recoup their cost.[115] They could not show their return on investment (ROI) to measure their research investment success.

When Dr. Campbell discovered that Ivermectin could be effective against the river blindness parasite, he got excited.

---

114 Emma Young, "River Blindness Breakthrough Offers New Hope," *New Scientist*, March 7, 2002.

115 Stephanie Weiss and David Bollier, "Merck & Company, Inc.: Having the Vision to Succeed," *St Andrew University*, accessed January 29, 2021.

His discovery could alleviate the suffering of millions of patients. He presented his idea to the head of the research lab. They concluded that it was unlikely that the drug would pay for itself.[116]

If the drug showed adverse effects on humans, the reputation of the drug would be tainted and sales of the drug for animals could fall. Alternatively, opportunists could smuggle the human version of the drug and sell it in the black market for animals, again undercutting Merck's sales.

Investing in curiosity and innovation is not the same as deciding whether a new manufacturing facility will yield success. Visibility into the future for each type of investment is different. The manufacturing facility requires a shorter time frame to yield results compared to research.

It did not make financial sense to continue the investigation of Ivermectin for humans. But curiosity was only one of Merck's cultural pillars; the other was to save lives.

George Merck, son of the company's founder, said, "We try never to forget that medicine is for the people. It is not for the profits. The profits follow, and if we have remembered that, they have never failed to appear. The better we have remembered it, the larger they have been."[117]

---

116 W. Michael Hoffman, Robert E. Frederick, Mark S. Schwartz, "Business Ethics: Readings and Cases in Corporate Morality" (5th ed), John Wiley & Sons, Inc. (2014).

117 Stephanie Weiss and David Bollier, "Merck & Company, Inc.: Having the Vision to Succeed," *St Andrew University*, accessed January 29, 2021.

As a business, Merck needs to make money. It needs to continuously develop and take new drugs to market to survive as a viable business. Success depended on a steady stream of innovations to stay ahead of the competition. Curiosity is their secret sauce to developing best-selling drugs.

But its mission is to save lives, not just the lives of the rich but also the poor. Merck already manufactured and sold Ivermectin as a treatment for animals. Iterating the product for humans would cost less than developing a drug from scratch.

In the end, the economic cost of developing the drug for humans did not outweigh the cost of human suffering. Merck could recoup the investment through the sale of other medications, the scientists reasoned. The Merck research team knew what they had to do.

Dr. Campbell followed his curiosity and worked to save others from suffering from the debilitating disease. Trial after trial proved successful, and WHO finally approved the drug for human use.

Then came the question of who would pay for the cost of production. Who would distribute it to the remote areas? The villagers suffering from the disease could not afford to pay for the drug. No public agency raised its hand to help and cover the cost.

Ultimately, Merck announced that they would distribute Ivermectin free to countries that requested it. During the thirtieth anniversary of the drug donation program, the company announced that it had successfully eliminated the disease in certain areas in the developing world.

Since the founding of the company, Merck's leadership has embedded curiosity and saving lives into its DNA. The Top Employers Institute recognized the company as a global top employer, particularly for their talent development and performance management.[118] Startups and corporations visit Merck's Innovation Center to learn about their culture of exploration. Almost 90 percent of their employees believe that curiosity is essential to addressing global problems.[119] Merck continues to introduce and manufacture best-selling pharmaceutical drugs and experience financial growth through its innovative culture.

INTELLECTUAL CURIOSITY

The Hershey Company was not Milton Hershey's first company. Not even his second. Hershey failed in his first two business ventures before he started his eponymous brand of chocolates. His curiosity led him to travel around the world and buy a German chocolate-making machine exhibited at the 1893 World's Columbian Exposition. With his new machine, he experimented with many products that led to quality chocolate confections and the Hershey's Kiss.[120]

This time, Hershey achieved great success. He built not only the largest chocolate factory at the time but also a

---

118 "Merck Named a Global Top Employer," *Merck,* February 6, 2019.

119 "2020 State of Curiosity Report: Survey Analyzes the Curiosity of Merck Employees," *Merck,* January 28, 2021.

120 "The Man Behind the Chocolate Bar," *Hershey Story,* accessed February 23, 2021.

community around the factory. He invested in residences and Hersheypark®, a family theme park for his employees. Most importantly, he established the Milton Hershey School, free for underprivileged lower-income children to attend. A trust containing most of Hershey's stake in his eponymous business funds the school. So if the Hershey business does well, the school receives more money to fund their operations.

Many years later, Bill Simpson, as President and CEO of The Hershey Entertainment and Resorts Company, made curiosity a part of his team's culture, and the Milton Hershey School his team's purpose.

Simpson was always a hard worker. He excelled in university and secured himself a spot in a management trainee program at a hotel group. He was excited about his career in the hospitality industry and jumped at every learning opportunity.

However, in the first half of his career, he got frustrated with the leaders he met and reported to. One of them lacked empathy, and another cared more about the profitability of his hotels than the welfare of Simpson or the rest of the team who had put in extra time. A third disrespected his team and did not develop his team members to their full potential. Each of these encounters left Simpson discouraged and unmotivated at work.

Still, Simpson pursued his career in hospitality and progressed to a leadership position, as the general manager of The Hershey Lodge. An encounter with a manager made Simpson realize that he was not yet fully equipped for the role.

At the Hershey Lodge, he developed a daily routine to review operations and stepped in to help where needed. This made his team members feel redundant—they felt that Simpson was micro-managing them. Instead of empowering his team to do their job, he would step in and take care of things himself. This was not what was required of him in his current role.

Like his previous managers, Simpson had the technical knowledge to manage operations and get the job done, but not the necessary leadership skills. Though he excelled as an individual performer, he had not evolved in his role to lead others. He was disappointed in himself.

Simpson went to work immediately. First, he enlisted the Human Resources department to design a training program for himself and the team collectively. He brought in James Hunter, author of *The Servant: A Simple Story about the True Essence of Leadership*, to teach the team about putting others' needs first. The author also encouraged them to keep learning. Hunter's ideas set Simpson's team into motion to seek improvements in their work.

Simpson also relied on his executive coach to guide him in his learning journey. But it takes a long time to break a bad habit. When Simpson slipped back into his old ways, his coach encouraged him to stay focused and try again. And with great courage and humility, Simpson acknowledged to his team what he needed to change in his leadership style and set out expectations for himself and the team. Simpson's willingness to continuously learn inspired his team to improve themselves too. He was their role model, and his humility gave them the space to make mistakes and get feedback for improvement.

As he advanced through the Hershey organization, Simpson continued to share his lessons with his team. He learned when leaders root their business in a core purpose, their employees become more inspired at work. At a team event, he led his team to discover their reason for existence: their core purpose was to support the Milton Hershey School. Their financial success results in expanding access to education.

His initiatives resulted in promotions, and employees moved across divisions that broke the silos previously there. Through these initiatives, employees developed better relationships within the organization and grew passionate and engaged at work. They also broke financial records despite the ambitious targets Simpson set for them. More students could attend the Milton Hershey School.

When a leader encourages curiosity and learning within his team, they are more adept at navigating through unchartered waters and develop better and more creative solutions. Curious teams are less prone to confirmation bias and, hence, will study information that supports and disagrees with their beliefs.[121] The additional data helps the team generate alternative ideas and make fewer errors in their solution design.

Curious employees tend to be more open-minded; instead of problems, they see opportunities to learn. In unpredictable

---

121 Anne-Laure Le Cunff, "Confirmation Bias: Believing What You See, Seeing What You Believe," *Ness Labs,* accessed February 22, 2021.

or new situations, these employees provide the team a sense of calm because they can better manage stress with the unknown.[122] They may even motivate others and get excited about having a problem to solve. Ultimately, this results in better team performance and resilience.

Related to that, we also enjoy working with curious coworkers. They are good listeners and have more empathy; they talk less and take an interest in our perspective. [123] They share their knowledge and inquire about what we think. Communication flows, and they deal with conflict better than others who focus on their perspective and insist on being right. Such behavior builds trust that results in more meaningful work relationships and collaboration within teams.[124]

When leaders reward their team on learning and personal growth, instead of cold hard performance metrics, team members become more motivated and engaged at work. These rewards respond to employee's needs to achieve their fullest potential. Employees who continuously learn at work often come up with improvement ideas however small they may be. They are less likely to fall into a routine or lapse into complacency because of the reminders to broaden their knowledge.

---

122 Todd B. Kashdan, Ryne A. Sherman, Jessica Yarbro, and David C. Funder, "How Are Curious People Viewed and How Do They Behave in Social Situations? From the Perspectives of Self, Friends, Parents, and Unacquainted Observers," *Wiley Online Library,* May 15, 2012.

123 Roman Krznaric, "Six Habits of Highly Empathic People," *Greater Good Magazine,* November 27, 2012.

124 Todd B. Kashdan and John E. Roberts, "Trait and State Curiosity in the Genesis of Intimacy: Differentiation from Related Constructs," *Guildford Press Periodicals,* June 2005.

THE BOTTOM LINE

- As we get older, we may lose our eagerness to learn and willingness to ask questions for fear of looking incompetent. We need to be aware of cognitive schemas that may contribute to stereotypes and prevent us from challenging the tried-and-tested ways of doing things.

- Dr. William Campbell at Merck combined his curiosity with the business purpose of saving lives to develop a cure for river blindness. Even though the manufacture and distribution of the drug did not earn the company any direct profit, Merck attracts the best talent with its culture founded on curiosity and purpose to save lives. Both factors enable the company to successfully develop and manufacture best-selling drugs.

- Bill Simpson nurtured a culture of learning at The Hershey Entertainment and Resorts Company that motivated his team to achieve financial success and their core purpose. Not only did he develop training and development initiatives, but he also role-modeled his willingness to learn. Investing in the training built better relationships within the team and increased engagement at work.

- The next chapter highlights some ways we can increase diversity of thought and perspective to become more creative at work.

REFLECT

1. List some areas that could benefit from increased creativity at work.
2. What may stand in the way of your challenging the status quo?
3. How could you be more curious at work?

4. What was the last thing in which you invested time to learn?
5. List at least five new topics about which you'd like to learn.

CHAPTER 8

BEING IN WONDER WITH THE WORLD

Popular belief recommends specialization for success. The more knowledge we gain in one area, the more likely we will meet fame and fortune.

But Bernice Eiduson found that Nobel prize-winning scientists were more likely than average scientists to have other interests. They were curious and independent thinkers.

They were not just scientists but also musicians, visual artists, poets, authors, and photographers. In her interviews with the Nobel laureates, they attributed their success to such pursuits, which opened their minds to fresh insight.[125]

Throughout the course of a typical day, the brain shifts between different concepts and may think about multiple

---

125 Waqas Ahmed, "This Is the Indispensable Skill That Will Future-Proof Your Career," *Fast Company,* June 16, 2020.

concepts simultaneously. This capability is known as cognitive flexibility.[126] The benefits of higher cognitive flexibility include the ability to acquire and integrate new information quickly, design creative solutions, and quickly adjust responses to changing situations. Individuals with greater cognitive flexibility tend to be more resilient and outperform their peers in dynamic situations.[127]

Architect Antonio Gaudi designed incredible buildings around Spain, many of which are in Barcelona. The most famous, La Sagrada Familia, towers above the trees and structures in Barcelona. His creative process inspires me.

Gaudi, a devout Catholic, loved nature, and these core sensibilities informed much of his work. For example, he used his observation of trees and developed the structure needed to hold up the towering La Sagrada Familia. He designed the internal columns of the cathedral to mimic the trees' overlapping branches, resulting in stable support for the cathedral and a design ahead of its time.

We recognize cognitive flexibility in polymaths, individuals who have knowledge in several unrelated areas. Some may call them generalists. Polymaths pursue their curiosity across diverse domains and can apply their rich knowledge base to design a creative solution. Polymaths who can and do apply their diversified knowledge on a specific problem are very valuable in teams. On the other hand, people who read across

126 KR Magnusson and BL Brim, "The Aging Brain," *Reference Module in Biomedical Sciences,* 2014.
127 Jennifer Verdolin PhD, "3 Ways to Improve Your Cognitive Flexibility," *Psychology Today,* December 3, 2019.

a range of subjects, but are unable to integrate or synthesize their learning, are merely walking encyclopedias.

Take Steve Jobs. He worked as a technician, made the first Apple computer, loved and obsessed over design, and audited a calligraphy class at Reed College. Combining the seemingly unrelated domains of typefaces and computer hardware birthed the beautiful, human-centric design of Apple computers. Cognitive flexibility empowered his imagination and creativity.

With the rapid change of technology and evolving customer expectations, we need cognitive flexibility to harmonize the needs of shareholders for profit and of employees and customers for engagement and loyalty.

Joseph DeSimone, cofounder of the 3D printing company Carbon, advocates for liberal arts education. A liberal arts education immerses students in a variety of subjects, ranging from science to arts. It trains them to think critically and practice ethical judgment, equipping them to be problem solvers in the workplace. Colleges encourage liberal arts students to pursue multiple interests, which cultivates a mindset for lifelong learning.

I had the chance to meet DeSimone during my time at adidas. Our company partnered with his to print sneaker midsoles, forging a partnership that enabled adidas to reduce environmental waste during production. Both Carbon and adidas shared the vision to reduce plastic use in the supply chain.

When the engineering team explained Carbon's revolutionary 3D printing technology, I was in complete awe. Other 3D printing technologies available in the market were essentially 2D, or traditional printing layered one on top of the other. Carbon's technology was inspired by the villain in *Terminator 2*, a character who rose from metallic puddles and shape-shifted at will. Similarly, Carbon's printers produce forms from liquid pools. This means that the printed result is a single form, which is critical to pass athletic footwear performance testing.

In addition to producing problem solvers, DeSimone believes that liberal arts training enables graduates to see around corners and predict not just immediate consequences but also subsequent effects of those actions. Change occurs more rapidly in the twenty-first-century economy, and lifelong learners look at new situations more critically and respond.

Looking ahead at Carbon's technology's potential, DeSimone decided to turn the 3D printing business model on its head. DeSimone is a liberal arts school graduate and a professor of Chemical Engineering at Stanford University. He set up a subscription business model where customers pay a fee to access technology, service, and support. Under the traditional printer model, customers purchase the printer and pay extra for support and upgrades. The Carbon model benefits the customer because they don't need to worry about upgrades. The printers are updated remotely, and there is no extra charge.

DeSimone was concerned that the technology he developed could be used for harm in the wrong hands. The terms of the subscription agreement prohibit the printers' use in the manufacturing of weapons. His breadth of knowledge across domains facilitated his second-order thinking—the ability to think deliberately past the immediate consequence.

To solve social and environmental issues, foster a culture of pursuing interests to develop cognitive flexibility. Form a learning habit. Encourage teams to immerse themselves in topics that interest them, even if these topics are unrelated to their work. Read about new science, business developments, and international news from multiple sources. These habits can enable the Altruistic Capitalist to solve wicked problems creatively.

CROSS-POLLINATION FOR DIVERSITY

Pixar Animation Studios, known for creative storytelling, produces award-winning movies, such as the *Toy Story* series, *Wall-E* and *Up*. Its secret lies in its culture and campus.

The Steve Jobs Building, home to Pixar, has an atrium in the center, lit during the day by natural sunlight. Bridges and stairs connect one section to another and bring the one thousand employees together.

After acquiring Pixar in 1986, Steve Jobs joined forces with Pixar cofounder Ed Catmull to build a creative culture founded on honesty and communication.

Jobs envisioned chance encounters between coworkers and wanted an office space that fostered those connections. Early design concepts featured a multi-structural compound, with scientists and animators in separate buildings. Jobs wanted everyone to work in one central space. So he designed the building for maximum chance encounters throughout the day: a single entrance and exit, a café and gym, and main restrooms located at the center atrium. You couldn't avoid having a conversation with someone if you worked there.

Catmull allowed employees to decorate their offices the way they wanted, encouraging self-expression, individuality, and creativity. Some offices resembled the front of a Western cowboy town and others had Hawaiian-themed offices. The Chief Creative Officer's work area was filled with plush toys from floor to ceiling.[128]

Pixar University, located on-campus, offers employees over one hundred free courses, ranging from filmmaking to drawing. Accountants and security guards, for example, could try things like drawing and other subjects that may be outside of their comfort zone.[129] The point of the courses was not to turn their accountants into artists but to encourage their employees to stretch their learning goals and look at the world differently. Breeding curiosity enabled teams to build broad networks and broke down silos in the organization.

Catmull did away with communication processes and allowed employees to approach anyone within the organization. There is no need to go through the proper channels

---

128 "Pixar Headquarters and the Legacy of Steve Jobs," *Office Snapshots*, accessed February 28, 2021.

129 William C. Taylor and Polly Labarre, "How Pixar Adds a New School of Thought to Disney," *The New York Times*, January 29, 2006.

to speak to anyone at Pixar.[130] If someone sees a problem, they should feel empowered to walk up to another person to work on solving it together. No one should wait for their manager to take action.

Respect and trust lie at the heart of Pixar's communication culture. In daily review meetings, employees give each other feedback to add to an idea, not to compete with it.[131] The focus and tone at the sessions are to make the end product better, not to tear each other down.

This free flow of communication is extended outside the company. Catmull pushed for Pixar to publish its findings and techniques, openly sharing the results of their experiments. This practice enabled Pixar to consistently attract top talent and build a community of people learning together in the industry.

Catmull attributed the success of Pixar's movies to the artistic and technical teams' seamless collaboration. One survey found 60 percent of respondents experienced a change in their way of thinking due to collaboration with their coworkers. Respondents who prioritized collaboration were also more likely to outgrow competitors.[132] Similarly, in driving our business toward delivering financial gain and a positive impact, we need business acumen, social impact know-how, and technical experts to design solutions together.

---

130 Ed Catmull, "How Pixar Fosters Collective Creativity," *Harvard Business Review*, September 2008.

131 Ibid.

132 "The Collaborative Economy," *Deloitte*, 2014.

We should be conscious of the subtle messages we deliver. What does the design of our workplace signal to our team? How do the communication practices affect creativity and collaboration? How can we inspire more trust and respect? We need to ask these questions when setting up our teams for curiosity and creativity.

CHECK YOUR ASSUMPTIONS AT THE DOOR

As leaders, we tend to rush to solve problems. People recognize us as successful when we break down complex issues and take them across the solution finish line.

But might we be reaching for solutions too quickly? What could happen if we allowed more space for exploration? What are the assumptions, misconceptions, stereotypes, and biases behind our answers when we rush to solve a problem? How do we know if these are true? When these assumptions are incorrect, what is the impact on the solution?

In a training program for Mars, Inc. executives, Cedric Bachellerie experienced the risk of relying on assumptions to solve problems. During the training program, the Mars team met with residents at risk of being displaced by gentrification in Cincinnati.

Squeezed into a community room, the trainer, Dr. Jane Craig, introduced the tenants' predicament to Bachellerie and the other Mars execs. Gentrification could mean access to improved health care, education, and safety. But the residents worried that gentrification would force them out of their homes. With increased gentrification in Cincinnati, the supply of low-income-affordable housing decreased.

After hearing the problem, Bachellerie rose to present his views on solving the problem. Having risen to senior ranks in innovation and marketing at Kimberly-Clark and Mars, he applied problem-solving frameworks he knew well. He sketched a few ideas and started to dive into each of them in more detail.

He was stopped mid-way by an older woman. She explained why his ideas would not work and what she and the other tenants had already tried. In her explanation, she exposed the incorrect assumptions that Bachellerie made in presenting his arguments.

The first step in solving a social problem is to frame the problem into questions. Why were the tenants opposed to the new developments in their area? What discussions and solutions had they tried? How did the gentrification process make them feel?

Bachellerie learned from the experience that we all have blind spots. We don't know what we don't know. He had not been in the tenants' position, at risk of being kicked out of his home. It was difficult for him to imagine what they were going through.

Bachellerie would have gained a better understanding of the tenants' perspective and experience if he'd tested his assumptions. He'd have been able to see the situation with fresh eyes and put himself in their shoes.

Dr. Craig, the trainer who designed the program, intentionally put Bachellerie and the other participants in a situation they would be completely unfamiliar with. The exercise highlighted that we all have preconceptions of the problem and the people experiencing them.

By shaking up the participants' status quo and putting them in a new situation, Dr. Craig proved that designing a social issue solution is not always obvious. We need to expose our assumptions and preconceptions and leave them at the door. Even within the same team, we walk in with our experiences and biases that cause us to see the situation differently.

We must be ready to get outside our comfort zone and step into the shoes of others. Ask questions such as:
- What are the gaps in our knowledge?
- Whose perspective are we missing?
- What specific circumstances do they face?

What is the issue defined at its simplest? Were the tenants worried they could no longer afford the rent in the area? Were they concerned with the increase in commercial activity that would impact their lifestyle and community? What resources are available? What did the developers want? What were they willing to work with? Knowing the issue and the right problem we are solving is half the battle won.

Asking these questions and listening to the answers with empathy increases our understanding of the plight of those suffering from the problem. With each response, we will reduce the ambiguity and gaps in our knowledge. This process also develops trust and openness in the relationship of everyone involved.

Once we have a full grasp of the situation, we can start to develop a solution based on facts rather than assumptions. We should also do this with all stakeholders. Having more people at the table has the advantage of having more ideas on the drawing board.

Don't edit the ideas at the beginning. Be curious about each one and wonder about them. Sharing ideas this way could refine some ideas and reveal the ones that would not work.

Be patient and understand that solutions don't work the first time. It is an iterative process. We have to be ready to debate and refine until all stakeholders are satisfied with the final answer.

THE BOTTOM LINE

- Polymaths have cognitive flexibility that enables them to design creative solutions using their diverse knowledge across domains. Examples of polymaths include Antonio Gaudi and Steve Jobs.
- Joseph DeSimone, founder of Carbon, believes liberal arts education trains students to think critically to be creative problem solvers in the long-term. The education also cultivates continuous learning in students that enables them to respond to new situations more effectively.
- Ed Catmull and Steve Jobs developed a creative culture at Pixar through intentional building design and open

communication, which fostered collaboration across the organization.

- Cedric Bachellerie learned the benefit of testing assumptions to discover his blind spots at a Mars, Inc. training program. We have to be prepared to step outside our comfort zone to design solutions that address the cause of the problem.
- We look at the mindset of athletes in the following chapter and discover how collaboration enables them to grow grit, persevere, and achieve their goals.

REFLECT

1. How could you practice a habit of lifelong learning?
2. How might you motivate yourself to maintain the habit?
3. Who can you enroll to help you identify your blind spots?
4. What might you do if you knew that you could not fail?
5. List a few things you would like to experiment with in the next month.

CHAPTER 9

THE MINDSET OF ATHLETES: GRIT

———

I have a fear of heights—which is why I thought it would be a good idea to learn how to boulder.

Bouldering is climbing without ropes or harnesses on rock formations or indoor artificial rock walls. I learned to boulder indoors. The walls averaged twenty feet (six meters), which is around four times my height.

Why did I do it? I was tired of feeling my stomach knot up when I looked down from tall places. So I took the leap and joined a local climbing gym.

The fifteen-foot-tall wall loomed before me. I gulped.

I've got this, I told myself.

I did the first few climbs without a hitch. Then I set my sights on a higher and more difficult wall. I slowly made my way up, feeling gingerly for each plastic-colored handhold and inching my feet into the wall surface's crevices.

I was about one move away from reaching the top of the wall. Suddenly, I became mindful of how high up I was. I looked down.

My stomach grew tight. I could hear my heart pounding in my head.

"You're almost there," the trainer urged me. "Just reach your right hand up to the next hold."

I remember my brain telling my right hand to lift itself just an inch, maybe lift up a finger. But I was frozen on the spot, paralyzed with fear. I couldn't imagine letting go of the safety net of that handhold to the next one. Intellectually, I knew it was just one move away. Mentally, I was a mountain away.

The best athletes are those who overcome their fear. Athletes fear losing a match, letting down their team, and not making their goals. Those who succeed get out of their comfort zone. Their passion for the sport, combined with their perseverance, enables them to become the best in their game. They have grit.

We admire athletes who make impossible shots and achieve godlike speeds. We don't see the hours of practice required to make that magic happen. They put in the effort day after day for the delayed gratification of achieving their dreams and goals.

To simultaneously create a positive impact and profit, we, too, must have grit. We must play the long game and persevere with passion.

GRIT AS A MARATHON, NOT A SPRINT

Leticia Galdón is the personification of grit. She cofounded Paz, a social enterprise that supports the integration of refugees into their new country. The company trains refugees in coding and web design so they can get jobs. After the refugees graduate from the program, Paz connects them with companies looking for tech talent.

When I met Galdón, I was humbled by her perseverance.

Asylum authorities and humanitarian agencies challenged Paz's work. Humanitarian agencies consider refugees as a vulnerable class of people who have nothing to offer the economy. Asylum authorities treat refugees with suspicion until their cases are accepted. When the authorities accept the refugees into the system, nonprofit organizations step in and support the refugees to integrate into the local community. This process often takes a long time, during which the refugees live in camps and are made to feel unwelcomed.

Paz challenges the status quo and argues that these refugees have something to offer. The organization helps this group of displaced professionals regain their self-esteem and self-worth. From the first day, the organization treats refugees with empathy and as people worthy of respect.

When Galdón tried to meet with refugees at the camps, government agencies and caseworkers turned her away. They did not believe the refugees had economic value to offer society.

Galdón finally got her foot in the door of a camp. She then had to convince the families, especially parents of girls, to trust her to teach their youth. Some humanitarian organizations saw their very existence threatened. If the refugees could get jobs and leave, these organizations would no longer serve any purpose. One organization even backed out on a Paz training program after months of planning and fundraising because they could not see a future beyond delivering what they were already delivering.

To gain the trust of the families, Galdón chose to live in a refugee camp and provide the training herself. During those months, she saw firsthand the disorientation and upheaval that came with the refugees being wrenched away from everything they knew, only to be looked at in contempt and treated like criminals upon arrival. This awareness led to a program design for a quick return to normalcy, starting with sustainable living wages.

Some nonprofit organizations saw her perseverance and wanted Galdón to work for them. She stuck with Paz because she believes in her mission to give the refugees independence, dignity, and the professional confidence they want. These were worthwhile sacrifices. Her dream is to scale the program and expand offerings to teenagers at the camps. These programs will help teenagers keep up with technological changes and integrate into their new home country. She envisions a diverse tech talent ecosystem where everyone feels accepted. This is Galdón's purpose. This is her marathon.

GENIUS BEHIND THE SCENES

Roger Federer finished 2020 ranked fifth in the top one hundred global rankings for professional male tennis. Having spent more than two decades on the professional circuit, he was also the oldest player in tennis's top one hundred. Federer's career accomplishments include a record twenty Grand Slam tournament wins and 310 weeks ranked number one in the world.

What does it take to sustain such high levels of performance in professional sports?

The average tennis serve is 145 mph (233 km/h). During play, tennis balls can clock in around 165 mph.

At those speeds, no one has time to think. Michael Jordan said, "Practice like you've never won." Success requires thousands of practice hours where no one is watching. Every practice shot matters as much as a competition shot. Even more importantly, the athlete who perseveres and wins is the one who repeatedly analyzes their mistakes and causes of failure.

As a long-time fan of the tennis maestro, I attribute Federer's longevity in the upper echelons of the sport to his passion and fierce commitment to improve. He made sacrifices and declined competitions and appearance fees. Not participating in competitions cost Federer ranking points. But this allowed him to preserve his thirty-nine-year-old body from the constant battery of playing on the circuit. He adapted his game according to changes in playing surface, and racket technology, just as his physical age started to show. If he hadn't reinvented his game, he would have struggled to keep up with younger players with higher physical endurance.

The young Federer in the late 1990s was a hot-tempered, pony-tailed teenager who smashed his racket. He cried over missed shots, slammed balls in anger, and whined about bad calls—behavior that worried his parents.

His coach at the time taught him the technical and mental skills needed to succeed in the sport. Being polite and gracious in defeat was the hallmark of champions—his tantrums were not. Federer's problem was his anger. When he got angry, he lost focus and his playing matched his mood—erratic and unpredictable.

Federer listened to the feedback and made it a point to "grow up." He shifted his mindset and worked with his team to grow stronger physically and mentally.

Fast forward twenty years later, his peers often describe Federer as the steely-cool, well-mannered sportsman on the court. His fans have seen the stoic Federer, down at match point, appear unruffled, his face betraying no emotion.

His graceful game and strategy to conserve his energy for lengthier plays marked an intentional shift from those tantrums of years ago.

"Learning from your mistakes is key, as we remember our losses more than our wins. It's just important that when you do lose, you really make the most of it because it's actually an opportunity," Federer reflected.[133]

We are not born with greatness. It took Federer years to cultivate and develop his emotional intelligence outside the court in order to face adversity on the court. Federer's investment in his learning has paid dividends in many victories and earned the respect of his peers.

MENTAL TENACITY

Zyrobotics founder Ayanna Howard worked hard for many years to achieve her dream. Her company develops educational products for students with disabilities to engage them in science and mathematics. The business is a culmination of her years working in artificial intelligence and human-robot interaction.

As a young student, Howard had a passion for robotics. Inspired by the television series, *The Bionic Woman*, she aspired to create bionic women who would do good for the world. At school, she took every opportunity to do extra work and pushed herself to learn more, especially in mathematics and physics.

When she headed to college, robotics degrees didn't yet exist. As an engineering major, she quickly learned she also needed

---

133 "Federer: 'I'm Not an Artist or A Musician,'" *ATP Tour* (blog), January 20, 2020.

mental tenacity to succeed. She often felt that she did not belong. But she stood her ground and graduated.

Still, when NASA assigned her to lead her first project at the Jet Propulsion Lab, Howard encountered unconscious bias. NASA assigned her as a team lead to develop artificial intelligence for future Mars rovers. When she entered the room, a male staffer barely looked up at her and said, "The secretaries work down the hall." He did not realize that Howard was his project lead.

Howard felt all the emotions we might expect—anger, fear, and uncertainty—yet she chose not to be controlled by those feelings. Instead, she channeled her energy into a positive response and focused on doing the work she needed to do.

Like Federer, her emotions were real, but she did not allow them to derail her. When we lead a purpose-driven business, we will face naysayers and others who disagree with our mission. We may feel beaten and discouraged. The outcome of our mission will depend on what we do with these feelings. To stay motivated, we can write down our purpose and mission and keep those close to us where we can see them easily. We can invest time to reflect in solitude, what has been done and what else needs to be done to achieve our purpose. Mindfulness helps us discern the difference between true feedback and negativity.

The development of Zyrobotics's product depends on feedback from customers and investors, some of which was less than encouraging. Howard advised that when working in innovation, the most important thing is to believe in yourself.

"There's always going to be someone who says, you can't do it or it's not going to work. You can't take it personally," she advised.

Ask for and remain open to conflicting feedback from different people. Look for patterns and identify feedback that recurs. When we validate feedback with mentors, we gain a more balanced perspective.

With experience comes the instinct to assess which feedback has merit and deserves consideration. When an investor asked Howard to pivot her business to cater to the mass market, her clear purpose helped her stay focused on her chosen niche market for students with disabilities. This conflict between listening to an investor and sticking to your guns happens to many entrepreneurs. Howard decided not to work with the investor. She found other investors who aligned with her purpose and helped her grow her business. "True success is reaching our potential without compromising our values," said Muhammad Ali, an American professional boxer.

"WE" NOT "ME"

Imagine a soccer game where everyone is running all over the field. Every player is fighting for ball possession, and there is no coordination. Chaos would reign. No one would score any goals.

Eleven players—including the goalkeeper—make up the team. The goalkeeper remains by his goalpost while the other ten players play in the defense, midfield, and forward areas of the pitch.

The forwards, also known as strikers, have the primary role of scoring the goals. And while they often get the most attention on the field, they can't strike without the others on the team. Midfielders play an equally important role to support both the forwards and defenders—striking when an opportunity opens up or acting as the first line of defense.

To win a game, one team must prevent the opposing team from scoring a goal. To do that, the team needs a strong defensive line.

A team where everyone plays their role is a team united. And a team united is a successful team. The "tiki-taka" style of play, popularized at FC Barcelona (Barça), is founded on team unity.

Instead of players holding the ball, tiki-taka involves short passes and movements. The team keeps possession of the ball and patiently brings it to the opposition's goal. Tiki-taka requires players to work closely together. Every player must remain aware of his teammates' positions on the field to see passing opportunities.

Under this strategy, lone stars can't win. Players may need to let go of their personal aspirations and focus instead on supporting their teammates on the pitch. This style of play requires more patience and perseverance in contrast to the long-passes style of play. It is about "us" keeping the ball rather than "me."

Barça used the tactic successfully to win multiple championships, including La Liga and the UEFA Champions League between 2009 and 2011.

COLLECTIVE POWER

Chemu Langat, regional head of Medtronic Labs Africa, discovered the importance of partnerships when she worked on cardiovascular and cardiometabolic health solutions in Africa. Medtronic Labs is "a social business dedicated to expanding access to healthcare" particularly focused on noncommunicable diseases in lower- and middle-income countries.[134]

Early in the project, Langat and her team discovered that the challenges of poor control of hypertension and diabetes in Ghana were complex and the cause not solely due to technology access. They initially assumed the problem was affordable technology, so they thought their medical device expertise would help.

But through deep ethnography—hundreds of interviews with clinicians, nurses, community health workers, and patients—they reached a game-changing conclusion. Complications from heart disease in Ghana, they learned, stemmed from multiple barriers, including poor awareness, late diagnosis, badly designed longitudinal care system, and cost. As we identified in Chapter 8, Langat and her team asked many Why questions in their initial research, which tested their assumptions and refined their chronic care offering.

After they had identified the cause, it became clear to Langat and the team that they needed a multifaceted care model founded on partnerships throughout the health care value chain in the country. They needed to build relationships with multiple clinics, pharmacies, pharmaceutical manufacturers,

---

134 "About," Medtronic Labs, accessed February 7, 2021.

and local authorities. By understanding the barriers to care, and which stakeholders addressed each part of the care continuum, the team identified who they could expand synergies with.

For the partnership to work, she learned that she needed to find a shared interest between her team and the partner. Success required strategic alignment around organizational mission and vision. Although the end goals may differ for each partner and Medtronic, a sufficient overlap was needed in the work the respective teams did along the way. Such an overlap would incentivize collaboration across multiple constituents. Through the shared vision, they built open communication and trust.

A large part of Ghana's health care delivery system was under local and national government agencies with varying levels of oversight. Culture and different decision-making frameworks frustrated the team. Other times, Langat and her team encountered a lack of commitment. It took grit for her team to persevere and patiently build these relationships. Through it all, they kept an open-mind and remained flexible to build trust.

Langat also faced the risk of delay when government officials or regulations changed. She learned to build proof points and success stories to establish themselves as subject-matter experts in the region. She measured the impact of their work. Alliances with other health care providers formed mini-regional networks and boosted her credibility to ease the introduction with new partners.

These strategies helped Langat and her team scale the impact of their Empower Health solution across multiple countries. To date, twenty thousand patients are enrolled in their program after they screened over twenty-five thousand people. Some of their successes from 2020 include:

- Renewal of a public-private partnership between Medtronic LABS, Novartis Global Health, Kenya's Ministry of Health, and the County Governments of Makueni, Nyeri, and Kakamega
- Partnership with Johns Hopkins University, Kwame Nkrumah University, and four District Hospitals in Kumasi, Ghana to test the feasibility of nurse-led, mobile-health-enhanced interventions for patients with uncontrolled diabetes and hypertension
- Partnership with PATH, Kenya's Ministry of Health, and the county governments of Makueni on innovative digital health solutions to improve primary health care delivery for non-communicable diseases in Kenya during COVID-19
- Partnership with the Christian Health Association of Ghana, Ghana's second-largest health provider, to collaborate on building and scaling up an integrated health care model to address the rising burden of non-communicable diseases

The more partnership roots you plant, the higher the likelihood of success for collective social impact.

THE BOTTOM LINE

- Leticia Galdón, the founder of Paz, patiently worked at developing relationships with public and humanitarian organizations to deliver tech training programs to refugees. Her clarity of purpose helped her persevere toward her goals.

- Despite his many tennis records, Roger Federer remains humble and listens to feedback to adapt his game to changes in the sport. He worked hard to improve himself so he could continue to perform at high competition levels for a longer time.
- Ayanna Howard, the founder of Zyrobotics, learned to control her emotions and accept only constructive feedback that aligned with her purpose. Her passion for artificial intelligence and capacity for hard work helped her persevere through challenges.
- Chemu Langat at Medtronic Labs understood the importance of building partnerships in her project to improve cardiovascular health in Ghana. Each constituent in the health value chain has their specialized knowledge and role to play that can quickly scale the implementation of solutions.
- The next chapter looks at examples from companies that grew grit to achieve sustainable growth.

REFLECT

1. Identify when you displayed grit to achieve your goal.
2. What are your long-term goals?
3. What stands in your way of achieving these goals?
4. Who can you enroll to help you achieve these goals?
5. When have your feelings caused an undesirable outcome?

CHAPTER 10

GO THE DISTANCE LIKE AN ATHLETE

———

Paul Polman will not shy away from a challenge. Where other CEOs see an obstacle to work around, Polman sees a mountain, daring him to climb it. And climb he did. In 2005, Polman pushed himself to new limits to ascend Mount Kilimanjaro, the highest free-standing mountain in the world. His fellow climbers were blind. "Without collective action," he later wrote, "none of us will make it to the top."[135]

It took grit and collaboration to make that summit. Four years later, Polman would bring that lesson with him into a different kind of adventure.

As the newly appointed CEO of Unilever, Polman surprised investors with news that he would stop reporting quarterly earnings. Unilever is subject to European Union law, which

———

135 Paul Polman, "Without Collective Action None of Us Will Make It to the Top," *LinkedIn*, February 19, 2018.

does not require quarterly reporting. However, companies voluntarily provided quarterly guidance to investors as standard practice. Like Rose Marcario at Patagonia, Polman thought quarterly reporting focused investors and employees on short-term thinking metrics, such as share price. On his first day on the job, he had made a statement, albeit a measured one. Polman quipped, "The first day they hire you, they're not going to fire you."[136] He said so less with a twinkle-in-his-eye than with his no-nonsense, Dutch practicality.

And if that wasn't enough to rankle the investors, he also made it clear that he only wanted to work with investors who agreed to his long-term strategy. He dared stock speculators to take their money elsewhere if they didn't like what he planned to do. With that, Polman signaled the multiyear transformation to come, ruffled a few feathers, and sent the company's share price tumbling by 8 percent. [137] But he also attracted long-term investors who liked his boldness, his Daring Leadership.

A year into the job, Polman made another daring declaration. Unilever, he said, would double its business and halve the size of its environmental footprint.[138] Many investors doubted that Polman would make it to the top of this mountain. Unilever's legacy brands—Hellmann's, Magnum, Lux, and Sunsilk—had shown lackluster performance for the previous decade.

---

136 Lilian Cunningham, "The Tao of Paul Polman," *The Washington Post*, May 21, 2015.

137 Andy Boynton, "Unilever's Paul Polman: CEOs Can't Be *Slaves* to Shareholders," *Forbes,* July 20, 2015.

138 "Unilever Aims to Double Business, Whilst Reducing Environmental Footprint," *Unilever*, accessed February 7, 2021.

But Polman already knew he couldn't get there by grit alone. So he empowered his team and initiated collective action. After he identified the vision, he rallied the organization. Together, specialists in science, sustainability, sales, supply chain, and social impact came together to develop a plan to climb the mountain.

As the first step in Polman's strategy to unite his executives, he brought his executive team to Port Sunlight, the former home of Unilever's founder, Lord William Lever. He started his business with Sunlight Soap, brought soap to the masses, and built a sizeable empire with global brands such as Lux and Lifebuoy. He also built residences, a hospital, and recreational facilities for his employees, much like Robert Owen had done at his mill in New Lanark, Scotland. Lord Lever guaranteed wages and jobs during World War I and introduced pensions in the UK. He believed in shared prosperity.[139] He was an Altruistic Capitalist.

Polman used the Port Sunlight visit to empower and inspire his executives to drive the business transformation Unilever needed. With the tour of Lever's home, he showed his team they were part of a company deeply rooted in social good. The executives rediscovered their core values and identified their strengths. They got excited. They started developing their plan to turn the business around—you can't make it up that mountain unless you are excited and passionate about the journey. And excitement is contagious. When we work collectively, we grow our grit.

---

139 David Gelles, "He Ran an Empire of Soap and Mayonnaise. Now He Wants to Reinvent Capitalism," *New York Times*, August 29, 2019.

When we work with others, we don't miss our blind spots. Someone in the team lets us know we're going the wrong way—if they don't, the team expends valuable time and energy to bring us back on track. If one of Polman's executives suggests a sustainable but unworkable initiative, the others refine the idea until all their objectives are met. Relationships built on shared knowledge and accountability form teams more likely to persevere through their challenges. They are grittier.

The journey to their roots invigorated the executives, and collectively they hatched the ten-year Sustainable Living Plan. The team nailed down their purpose—to improve the health of one billion people and enhance the livelihoods of millions in their community.[140] But this was still not sufficiently granular or concrete for the team member doing their job on the ground. To move the entire organization in the same direction, they broke down their purpose into fifty time-bound goals.

Under health improvement, they included the provision of safe drinking water, access to sanitation, and reduction of respiratory disease through handwashing (a nod to Lifebuoy and the company's origins) within the goals. To enhance livelihoods, the team wanted to empower women through a more gender-balanced organization and enhanced access to training and skills. Anyone within the organization could pick up the plan and figure out what they should do to help the company up that mountain.

---

140 "Sustainable Living," *Unilever*, accessed February 7, 2021.

Polman paired clear ambitions with transparency and exposed areas where he had underestimated challenges. He published all the results and progress of Unilever's goals. For instance, their target was to train 5 million women, but they only managed to reach 2.2 million. Such misses opened their eyes to the lives of women farmers, and the barriers to education for them. No journey is lost if the lesson is learned and synthesized.

Transparency also attracted others outside Unilever to collaborate on the initiatives. For example, the company decided to publish the names of its suppliers. The decision to make their supply chain visible incentivized farmers, suppliers, and governments to promote sustainable practices and increase innovation within the supply chain. The publication of their suppliers pushed producers to achieve sustainable certification. The move also connected Unilever with like-minded buyers to achieve sourcing at scale of more sustainable raw materials.[141]

Polman wanted to reach one billion people through their health program by 2020. Unilever launched on-ground programs with mothers and children, built partnerships with local non-government organizations, and used modern storytelling to build awareness. It also mobilized youth networks and used mobile phones to connect with villagers in rural areas.[142] They brought collective action to their local communities and sparked change. His team achieved that goal by 2018.

---

141 "Lessons Learnt: Visibility Leads to Sustainable Sourcing," *Unilever*, accessed February 26, 2021.

142 "Healthy handwashing habits for life," *Unilever*, accessed February 26, 2021.

At the end of Polman's ten-year tenure, Unilever returned 290 percent to its shareholders and grew its market share in emerging markets.[143] Share price more than doubled when Polman was at the helm. He achieved strong results through financial discipline and value maximization for all stakeholders. He acquired brands such as Seventh Generation and TAZO® tea, which focused on sustainability. Conversely, he fended off a takeover attempt by Kraft Heinz. He feared for their opposing cultures and particularly for Kraft Heinz's detachment from sustainability.[144] He wanted to grow the business and still halve the environmental footprint of its business.

Polman met his goal of growing the business by increasing the number of Sustainable Living Brands, such as Dove and Ben & Jerry's. These brands "communicate a strong environmental or social purpose, with products that contribute to achieving the company's ambition of halving its environmental footprint and increasing its positive social impact."[145] Unilever's Sustainable Living Brands grew 69 percent faster than the rest of the business, which demonstrated the financial potential of purpose-driven brands.

Polman's success in turning around the ninety-year-old company speaks volumes to the possibilities that the collective can achieve with grit.

---

143 "Unilever CEO Announcement: Paul Polman to Retire; Alan Jope Appointed as Successor," *Unilever,* November 29, 2018.

144 David Gelles, "Paul Polman, a 'Crucial Voice' for Corporate Responsibility, Steps Down as Unilever C.E.O.," *New York Times,* November 29, 2018.

145 "Unilever's Purpose-Led Brands Outperform," *Unilever,* June 11, 2019.

PROGRESS AND FEEDBACK

Athletes meticulously measure their progress. They track speed, time, weight lifted, distance covered, and heart rate response and recovery to assess if they are on track with their training goals. A good coach trains the athlete holistically, physically, and mentally to achieve the desired outcome. This includes education about nutrition and learning to listen to the athlete's body for rest and recuperation. Too often, we push our bodies to train faster and harder, resulting in an injury that could lead to long-term damage. While we may run faster today, not taking a day of rest could mean we may not run effectively in the future.

In sports, sometimes we also need to pause and reflect on what is working and what is not. Instead of blindly following a training plan, check in to see if the plan is the right one for us. If we are putting in the effort but not making progress, ask why.

Set up a system to measure the right data points correctly. Data points could include general health indicators such as sleep, nutrition, and energy levels. Manual inputs of data and inaccurate fitness trackers lead to inadequate measuring systems. It's frustrating for the athlete when data is flawed. Even when data may be less than perfect, they give us a sense at least of whether we are going in the right direction. Accurate data points serve as feedback for the athlete. Together with their trainer, the athlete can translate these data points into insight and determine how best to level up their game and reach their goals.

Similarly, after setting up our mission and time-bound goals in business, we need to design a system to capture data points to measure progress. The other half of the equation is to analyze the data, determine the corrective action, and incorporate it into our work. This then restarts the feedback loop process.

Purpose-driven businesses need to design a system to measure progress and gather feedback to manage their stakeholders' shared goals and interests. As leaders, we need to ask what stakeholders we need to involve. Other considerations include the frequency and depth of contact (in-face meeting versus email). Information that may be relevant for investors may not be as interesting for customers or the community. Employees' and vendors' feedback may be more influential in supply chain decisions, compared to customers who may influence product development decisions.

Sustainability investors use ESG (environmental, social, and governance) ratings and reports from third-party providers to evaluate a public company's performance compared to its peers. Analysis of such reports could cause an investor to divest from a company where it does not meet ESG standards. This is an opportunity for business leaders to engage in a dialogue with their investors, build a more open relationship, and get feedback.

Openness and transparency are critical for the feedback progress to work. Savannah Johnson, who worked at Harlem Capital, firmly believes that people should critically examine collectively what is being done and why. Then they should ask, how does this move the needle toward making an impact. Harlem Capital is a venture capital firm that invests in women and minority entre-preneurs who often have trouble raising financing for their businesses.

The firm systemizes feedback into its business practice. Every week, the entire firm spends two hours together to review their feedback document. The fifteen-member firm updates this document throughout the week, with comments on what went well and possible improvements.

The weekly open forum embeds self-reflection and challenges each team member to think about what they could do better. The atmosphere is collaborative and transparent. Everyone is there to help each other learn, which also leads to better business decisions.

Rather than anonymous or closed-door feedback processes, this system fosters open discussion and collective learning. The document also serves as a record so that others may learn from what the group discussed previously.

Although this process may not be scalable at a larger orga-nization, the concept could be replicated. Teams should design a process that works for them. Ed Catmull at Pixar organized daily review meetings. These sessions increased creativity and innovation across the whole team and ensured the team focused on the areas that needed improvement.[146] When applied to solve an intractable problem, feedback can help a team persevere.

---

146 Ed Catmull, "How Pixar Fosters Collective Creativity," *Harvard Business Review*, September 2008.

TEAM AND TRANSPARENCY

Merino wool. Eucalyptus. Sugar cane. Castor bean oil.

You wouldn't expect to find these materials in a sneaker. But the Allbirds Tree Dasher, a running sneaker, is unlike many other running sneakers that rely on oil-based synthetics like plastics.

Tim Brown wanted a sneaker that was not overly designed with logos and was friendly to the environment. So he started Allbirds, a direct-to-consumer sustainable sneaker company. Brown has many of the Altruistic Capitalist's characteristics we've examined. The first sneaker resulted from his curiosity: Could sneaker designs be simpler, have fewer colors, and be minimalistic? Why don't footwear companies use merino wool in uppers for sneakers? Could we have a running shoe that could be worn sockless?

Along the path to cofounding a high-end sneaker company, Brown wore out a lot of sneakers on the soccer field. As vice-captain of the New Zealand team, he learned a lot about team chemistry. So when the time came to build the company culture, he sought to replicate the culture that led to his soccer team's wins. Employees should eschew their egos and build teamwork and collaboration.[147]

Instead of the usual single chief executive, Brown shares the company's reins with Joey Zwillinger, the other co-CEO of the business. Building a sustainable footwear business is

147 Cameron Albert-Deitch, "Comfy Shoes Helped Allbirds Become a $1.4 Billion Company, but It's Never Been Just About Shoes," *Inc.*, December 4, 2018.

complex, and Brown did not have the experience or skill set to establish a stable supply chain.

Brown realized the value of the partnership with Zwillinger, an industrial engineer and a renewable materials expert. Brown brought his sports industry and design knowledge to the equation. It was a symbiotic relationship, with neither having the final veto on decisions. Both agreed that this was a partnership where they could go further together than apart.

Brown said of Zwillinger, "I found in him a partner. Someone to laugh through the challenges of doing this, someone with a complementary set of skills, but perhaps most importantly, (someone with a shared) purpose around sustainability."[148]

The co-CEO organization structure sets the tone for humility and partnership in the office. Allbirds has a healthy diversity hiring practice and encourages employees to challenge ideas. Each member of the team is respected for the unique value they bring. The glue that brings them together is their shared purpose.

Their belief in the power of the collective led them to build partnerships outside the company. When the duo started the business, they knew their sneaker was not as sustainable as it could be. Like many sneakers, the original Allbirds' foam bottom used petroleum.

---

148 Jason Buckland, "Tim Brown on Co-CEOs at Allbirds, and Leaving No Carbon Footprint Behind," *ShopifyPlus*, January 5, 2021.

They worked closely with a manufacturer for a few years to develop a foam bottom made mainly of sugarcane. The result was a patented composite material that Allbirds called SweetFoam.

Instead of keeping SweetFoam to themselves, they released the formula to the public so others could use the eco-friendly material as well. [149] It is an open invitation to their peers to join their effort to reduce carbon emissions into the environment.

Transparency brings teams together. Like Polman, Brown, and Zwillinger believe in communication for better alignment. There are regular updates from board meetings and on business progress. After every board meeting, the co-CEOs gather the entire company at a roundtable to dissect what happened. Every other week, the pair shares positive and negative business developments. Then there is a monthly companywide newsletter to share what Brown and Zwillinger have on their minds.[150]

Zwillinger set up metrics to measure the carbon footprint at each stage of their products. These metrics, named KIWIs ("keep improving with intent"), in a nod to Brown's heritage, tracks emissions at the supply chain, production, and retail operations. KIWIs are looked at alongside the company's

---

149 Cameron Albert-Deitch, "Comfy Shoes Helped Allbirds Become a $1.4 Billion Company, but It's Never Been Just About Shoes," *Inc.*, December 4, 2018.

150 Cameron Albert-Deitch, "A Decade Ago, He Helped Lead New Zealand to the World Cup. Now, Allbirds's Founder Is Bringing Those Team-Building Lessons to His Company," *Inc.*, September 17, 2019.

priorities, to come up with individual employee objectives. Every objective and metric are tracked and measured in an online software tool for visibility and seamless integration.[151] It also helps employees to see how their effort directly contributes to making a carbon-neutral product.

They kicked transparency up a notch with their carbon label. These labels inform the consumer of the carbon footprint of the product.[152] Just like Patagonia's Black Friday ad campaign, *"Don't Buy This Jacket,"* this was a courageous and audacious move. The label has twin objectives. The company challenged its peers to disclose the carbon footprint of their products too. But the other objective was to challenge themselves, to remind the team how much more they would need to do to get to carbon neutral (which is their ultimate goal).

They are not carbon neutral yet. But they continue to invest in research and grow partnerships to get there. Like other founders of purpose-driven companies, Brown and Zwillinger know that they can't get to the perfect solution on Day One. They have to work with existing market conditions. In the meantime, they continue to produce and sell their sneakers, while introducing improvements one step at a time. But until they reach their goal of net-zero emissions, Allbirds tax themselves for their carbon emissions (it appears as an expense on their financial statements) and fund projects that neutralize their footprint.[153]

151 Evan Schwartz, "Anchoring OKRs to Your Mission," *What Matters*, June 26, 2019.
152 Lela London, "Allbirds Is the First Fashion Brand to Label Its Carbon Footprint Like Calories," *Forbes*, April 15, 2020.
153 "Sustainability," *Allbirds*, accessed March 3, 2021.

The enormity of the mission does not stop the Altruistic Capitalist. They may have to make trade-offs throughout their journey, whether it is at the sacrifice of profit or purpose. What matters is the accumulation of knowledge to move them in the right direction of purpose. "Wisely and slow, they stumble that run fast," Friar Laurence warned Romeo in William Shakespeare's *Romeo and Juliet*. On the road to building prosperous and sustainable businesses, it pays to go slowly and intentionally today to go the distance tomorrow.

THE BOTTOM LINE

- Paul Polman, as CEO of Unilever, set the business a clear ten-year mission, which was broken down into measurable time-bound goals. By publishing progress on these goals, he brought transparency to internal and external stakeholders. He successfully grew the business while reducing its environmental footprint through bold ambitions and perseverance.
- Capture data and collect feedback to measure our progress toward our goals. Systemize feedback and nurture open communication to ensure the process is additive to reaching long-term targets.
- Tim Brown and Joey Zwillinger, cofounders of Allbirds, founded their company culture on collaboration and transparency. They published the formula to a patented sustainable material they developed and label their products with their carbon footprint. Such moves remind them, their employees, and customers of their ultimate mission to get to carbon neutral.

- The final chapter of *The Altruistic Capitalist* brings together the three mindsets of mindfulness, curiosity, and grit. It also looks at what's in-store for purpose-led businesses.

REFLECT

1. When was the last time you asked for feedback? What made it an effective or ineffective learning opportunity?
2. How might you systemize feedback and capture your progress?
3. List specific questions you would like to address in the feedback session.
4. What areas of communication need improvement?
5. Identify ways to increase transparency in communication.

PART III

GROUNDED IDEALISM

Yesterday is not ours to recover, but tomorrow is ours to win or to lose.

PRESIDENT LYNDON B. JOHNSON

CHAPTER 11

WHAT LIES AHEAD

———

The Altruistic Capitalist is about building business as a force for good. The current state of global warming and social problems such as rising income inequality screams at us, "Take action now!" Acting in the obsolete profit-maximizing way contributed to this mess in the first place. We can't continue to lead our companies from that perspective.

It would be unethical to leave governments and nonprofit organizations to clean up the mess. Business has a social responsibility to reduce the damage and instability in our environmental and social ecosystem, and we cannot lead from the backseat.

We must start by shifting our leadership mindset. Profit maximization and financial rigor should be accompanied by a more humane approach to leadership. Business leaders can drive change by:
- Building a culture and incentives conducive to create sustainable prosperity
- Inspiring others through clear communication and example

- Rallying their peers and teams using a shared purpose and vision
- Innovating their business models
- Empowering others to realize the vision

The Altruistic Capitalist mindset provides leaders with models to think about their businesses. The three protagonists— the Monk, the Five-Year-Old, and Athletes—each have their own superpower and can see the world in their unique way. Athletes think in goals and grow their grit to achieve their fullest potential. The Five-Year-Old thinks in questions and may challenge the validity of those goals. The Monk reflects: Are they on the right path of purpose to start with?

The three protagonists provide a complete and holistic approach to business. The first mindset, mindfulness, grounds a leader in purpose, their reason of existence. When a leader has a high level of self-knowledge, they have higher humility and become more empathetic. This leader will likely set up an organizational purpose that considers the business's impact on their stakeholders: employees, suppliers, customers, investors, and the environment.

Robert Iger at The Walt Disney Company made decisions unequivocally that could have resulted in a negative financial impact. Had he been focused on profit maximization like Travis Kalanick at Uber, he would have made entirely different decisions. Iger's consistency in deciding according to his purpose produced healthy financial outcomes for the business.

The second mindset, curiosity, requires us to ask "Why?" and "Why Not?" of assumptions. By embracing a love for learning, we become comfortable with uncertainty and can move away from old practices and ways of thinking. An emphasis on continuous learning at a company like Hershey can help solve problems more frequently and effectively when change threatens the existence of its business.

During COVID-19, restaurants were either forced to close or open at reduced capacity. The more creative restaurants pivoted. They offered their customers prepared meal kits and grocery delivery services that enabled them to continue paying their employees and support their customers through a stressful time. Curious leaders have high resilience to manage environmental and social problems that force businesses to change.

The third mindset, grit, builds partnerships and networks to persevere through problems. We multiply our impact when we share our knowledge and resources with others. Chemu Langat at Medtronic Labs worked closely with her partners to overcome issues and stay on track with her team's goals.

Profit-maximizing companies tend to be lone wolves, an environment rife with competition. Before Satya Nadella's arrival, Microsoft's teams did not trust each other, and internal fights and power plays consumed teams' energies. The business lagged behind its competitors, including Apple and Google. Nadella transformed Microsoft's culture into a more collaborative one by leading with empathy and humility.

The three mindsets—mindfulness, curiosity, and grit—go hand in hand. Leaders behind profitable and sustainable businesses set their sights on longer-time horizons compared to their profit-maximizing peers. The mindsets provide the bedrock for the Altruistic Capitalist to achieve their goals.

Fundamentally, the Altruistic Capitalist is humble. Through regular reflection, they can see their competitive advantage and their flaws. This leads them to develop open and trustworthy partnerships with others to achieve shared goals. They admit their mistakes and design feedback systems to improve themselves continuously. They invest in the business of relationships and are less interested in accepting glory for themselves.

WHAT LIES AHEAD

Companies will experience many governance changes in the short to medium term. In September 2020, the World Economic Forum (WEF) published a metrics reporting guide to measure businesses' environmental, social, and governance standards. The Stakeholder Capitalism metrics cover:

- Principles of governance, such as purpose and accountability
- Planet, such as greenhouse gas emissions and water consumption
- People, such as diversity and inclusion, and training
- Prosperity, such as employment and taxes paid[154]

---

154 "Measuring Stakeholder Capitalism: Toward Common Metrics and Consistent Reporting of Sustainable Value Creation," *World Economic Forum,* September 2020.

These metrics show how a company's activities affect the environment, and people: everything is connected. The connection had been missing from financial statements. For example, when a company depletes water resources in a community, quality of life and potential livelihood suffer. Such situations raise questions about accountability, and the governance to prevent such situations.

The metrics nudge companies toward creating long-term value for their customers, community, and investors. The WEF gathered feedback from investors, regulators, and corporations to develop the metrics. The framework received strong buy-in from participants who came from different industries, including mining, and oil and gas.

Four months later, the WEF published the Value Creation Governance, a practical guide to establish oversight into an organization's activities. Recommendations on incentives and board composition focus the executive on value creation, not on shareholder returns alone. This leads to better decision-making for a prosperous and sustainable business.[155]

At the time of publication, the Stakeholder Capitalism metrics and Value Creation Governance are only recommendations, the implementation of which are voluntary. In concert with global standard setters, the WEF's development of a corporate reporting system continues. By embedding the Stakeholder Capitalism metrics in companies' operations, it may soon make it mandatory for businesses to focus on

---

155 "The Future of the Corporation: Moving from Balance Sheet to Value Sheet," *World Economic Forum*, January 2021.

social impact. Investors may start to allocate their money based on these metrics. This could lead to good and better corporate citizens.

When some large corporations start publishing their social impact metrics, their peers may have to answer to their investors and customers, "What are they hiding?" Metrics transparency may lead to setting clear improvement targets, prioritizing the most urgent issues in front of the CEO. The intention is not to villainize any company but to help lift each other up and create a more sustainable world for everyone.

FIRST THINGS FIRST

To grow into an Altruistic Capitalist, one first needs to know where they stand with the three mindsets. How mindful are you? How curious are you? How gritty are you?

STEP 1: SELF-EXAMINATION

I've included the **Altruistic Capitalist Self-Assessment** in the Appendix to help you identify areas for improvement and evolution.

STEP 2: PURPOSE

Work through the Reflect section, particularly the questions in Part II, to identify your purpose and core values.

STEP 3: AMBITION

State your ambition. Paul Polman's ambition was to double Unilever's business and halve its environmental footprint. Break down the ambition into no more than five time-bound goals. Having too many goals divides your attention. Each additional item lessens the priority of the others; you won't achieve more by listing more goals, you will just end up with many unfinished projects.

STEP 4: RELATIONSHIPS

Deepen your relationship with peers, mentors, and team members. Build a community around your journey. Share your purpose and goals with the community. Ask them for ideas and what they'd like to achieve. Find areas of commonality and develop a shared vision to support each other.

For teams, develop an action plan for the team that aligns with the collective group's purpose and goals.

Check in regularly to offer encouragement and celebrate each other's progress.

STEP 5: KNOWLEDGE

During the check-ins, request specific feedback to identify your blind spots and identify ways for improvement. Develop a thirst for knowledge. Maintain a Knowledge Journal, where you track your progress and record lessons learned from reflections and conversations with others.

The check-ins may reveal more information (to add to the Knowledge Journal) that requires the repetition of Steps 2 and 3. The steps may be repeated until the ambition is reached. The cycle starts again with a new ambition.

* * *

Changing our beliefs and mindsets is a journey that can't be achieved overnight. Be patient and intentional with practice. Worthy ambitions take time to bear fruit. Leaders should empower their teams and set up succession plans so that the work they started may persist beyond them.

Each of us has the power to propel the movement. The choices we make compound. We will not notice the daily 1 percent improvement, but over the course of 365 days, we will end up thirty-seven times better than when we started.[156] For example, if we start with two minutes of meditation on day one, and we increase by 1 percent each day, we will meditate for two minutes and seven seconds on day seven (a barely noticeable difference). If we continue to increase the time by 1 percent each day, we would meditate for almost seventy-five minutes by the end of the year. The purpose of this example is to illustrate the power of continuous learning and deliberate daily practice. There may be days when we falter and fall—what matters is getting up and trying again. Confucius said, "The man who moves a mountain begins by carrying away small stones."

We can collectively build a better world if we each take a step forward every day.

---

156 James Clear, "Continuous Improvement: How It Works and How to Master It," *James Clear* (blog), accessed March 1, 2021.

THE ALTRUISTIC CAPITALIST SELF-ASSESSMENT

———

I developed this self-assessment to support leaders in their Altruistic Capitalist learning journey. Like the planet, the public perception, and the people around us, we are constantly evolving. As such, the results from the assessment below should not be taken as fixed. They should be used as a gauge of the current state.

There are no right and wrong answers. Just answer honestly and take into consideration how you perceive yourself in comparison to others.

For each statement, assess whether you exhibit the behaviors **Often**, **Sometimes**, or **Rarely**.

HOW MINDFUL ARE YOU?

1. I remain calm and objective when faced with disruptive events or emotional triggers.
2. I can stay present, focus on tasks, and ignore modern-day distractions from my phone or social media.
3. I observe situations without assigning labels, values, or judgment.
4. I am fully aware of my actions and try not to behave on autopilot.
5. I set aside time for reflection.

HOW CURIOUS ARE YOU?

1. I like to test out new ideas to see how things will turn out.
2. I am excited about learning new subjects and developing new skills.
3. I ask questions before embarking on a project.
4. I challenge tried-and-true methods.
5. I am comfortable with uncertainty.

HOW GRITTY ARE YOU?

1. I set long-term goals for myself.
2. I start whatever I finish.
3. When I struggle with a project, I will ask for help and not give up.
4. When I make a mistake or fail, I ask for feedback to improve.
5. In a team, I am clear about my role and fulfill my responsibilities.

At the end of the Self-Assessment, look back at the statements answered with **Sometimes** or **Rarely**. These indicate areas for improvement. The Self-Assessment can be used again whenever time calls for another pulse check.

ACKNOWLEDGMENTS

—

To my dearest family:
I'm blessed by your unconditional love and support that shaped who I am today.

To my loyal group of friends who cheered me on:
I'm indebted for the weekly walks, Zoom calls, and messages to make sure that I made it through this journey alive.

To the New Degree Press team:
I'm thankful for the advice and quick responses at all hours of the day to bring this book to life. Special thanks to Pea Richelle While for her creative guidance.

To Bill Simpson, Mary Ann Tate, Shaun Tracey, and Stela Zarija:
My utmost appreciation for your dedication to point out my blind spots in early drafts.

To the people I met and whose stories I shared throughout this book:

I'm very grateful for your work and leadership, to make the world a better place. Thank you for the inspiration.

Especially for my early supporters:
Thank you for spreading the word, supporting the project, and preordering *The Altruistic Capitalist*. This dream came true because of you.

With all my gratitude.
Yap Fung Kiat & Teh Yoke Hoe, Yap Jen Min & Jennifer Lee, Andrew Maywah, Dato' Teo Chiang Quan, Laurent Godfroy, Lee Peng Keong, YAM Tunku Ali Muhriz, Ng Thin Huatt & Teh Geok Lian, Goh Hooi Theng, Han Chun Lim & Christina Ma, Maxime Gorillot, Teh Yoke Keng, Bryon Graulich, Igli Gjozi, Matt Jacob, Adelyn Koh, Brendan Jayagopal, Diana Kates, Jo & Dave Williams, Raghu Yabaluri, David Bell, Derik Zusann, Isaac Esseku, John Paul O'Meara, Lindsay Main, Ruben Millan Alonso, Victor Gaspar, Simon Berle, Don Hatch, Aileen Chua, Arasendran Indrasith, Arlene Khaw, Aude Germanier, Cedric Bachellerie, Dahlia Bock, David Rubinow, Ethan Piper, Hanyi Lim, Hiew Chee Faun, Jack Spencer and Jun Pang, Jen Baughan, Kevin King, Moritz Ostermayer, Sanjeev Singh, Sara Fleming, Si Chay Beng, Tay Hong Peng, Teh Lei Choo, Teh Sam Moy, Teh Say Yan, Teh Yoke Hooi, Teh Yoke Kuan, Yau Chung Ng, Adrien Carnemolla, Alessandro Paoli, Alexandra Meier, Alice Lonardi, Andreas Lorenz, Angeline Schmid-Egger, Benjamin Castro, Boris Djordjevic, Casey Ames, Elisabetta Baroldi, Elvina Chu, Erwan Berthelot, Fabrice Atallah, Florian Hofmann, Hamilton Perkins, Helena Francis, Jarret A. Schlaff, Jeffrey Michel, Jennifer Lee, Jin Sheen Yeoh, Jiraindira Purushothaman, Jordi Bartual Paris, Jordi Serrano

Pons, Justin Polgar, Justina Markeviciene, Karen Kimkana, Karen Kranack, Karim Yehia, Lily Shapiro, Lindsey McCoy, Marisol Giacomelli, Matthias Koehler, Nan Fen Teh, Petar Mitrovic, Santosh Sahoo, Sebastian Schneider, Tanya Alvarez, Teresa Salazar, Vicente Calatayud, Vicki Moore, Adrian Lim, Annemiek Timmerman, Arianna Cavallo, Dave Chae, Deborah Li, Dimitri Yang, Edward Stoner, Emmanuel Kostucki, Goh Chee Leong, Hannah Gabriel, Kara Brody, Kathleen Sek, Kunal Nandy, Lim Tek Wee, Liz Oswald, Loo Chi Meng, Low Kar Chuan, Lynn Han, Martin Sieg, Natthorn Chaiyapruk, Raad Salman, Ross Dakin, Sheezan Bakali, Stela Zarija, Susanne Dolderer, Taketo Yasu, Victoria Masters, Vinita Chhay, Vishnu Veerubhotla, Wan Yin Chan, Yap Li Peng, Ye Qian, Yuanfang Yan, Matthias Wirth.

BIBLIOGRAPHY

———

INTRODUCTION

Hale, Jon. "Sustainable Equity Funds Outperform Traditional Peers in 2020." *Morningstar*, January 8, 2021. https://www.morningstar.com/articles/1017056/sustainable-equity-funds-outperform-traditional-peers-in-2020.

Schwartz, Tony. "Companies That Practice Conscious Capitalism Perform 10x Better." *Harvard Business Review*, April 4, 2013. https://hbr.org/2013/04/companies-that-practice-conscious-capitalism-perform.

Whelan, Tensie and Carly Fink. "The Comprehensive Business Case for Sustainability." *Harvard Business Review*, October 21, 2016. https://hbr.org/2016/10/the-comprehensive-business-case-for-sustainability.

CHAPTER 1

Baer, Drake. "Patagonia CEO: 'There's No Way I Should Make One Decision Based on Quarterly Results.'" *Business Insider*, November 19, 2014. https://www.businessinsider.com/patagonia-ceo-interview-2014-11.

Banks, John P. "Millennials and the Future of Electric Utilities." *Brookings, Planet Policy* (blog), July 11, 2014. https://www.brookings.edu/blog/planetpolicy/2014/07/11/millennials-and-the-future-of-electric-utilities/.

Beer, Jeff. "EXCLUSIVE: Patagonia CEO Rose Marcario Is Stepping Down." *Fast Company*, June 10, 2020. https://www.fastcompany.com/90515307/exclusive-patagonia-ceo-rose-marcario-is-stepping-down.

Business Roundtable. "Business Roundtable Redefines the Purpose of a Corporation to Promote 'An Economy That Serves All Americans.'" August 19, 2019. https://www.businessroundtable.org/business-roundtable-redefines-the-purpose-of-a-corporation-to-promote-an-economy-that-serves-all-americans.

Coates, Sam. "Verdict on Capitalism: Unfair and Corrupt." *The Times,* November 3, 2015. https://www.thetimes.co.uk/article/verdict-on-capitalism-unfair-and-corrupt-w6t5q7q52kq.

Dimock, Michael. "Defining Generations: Where Millennials End and Generation Z Begins." *Pew Research Center.* Accessed January 29, 2021. https://www.pewresearch.org/fact-tank/2019/01/17/where-millennials-end-and-generation-z-begins/.

Edelman. "2020 Edelman Trust Barometer." January 19, 2020. https://www.edelman.com/trust/2020-trust-barometer.

Ehrenfreund, Max. "A majority of Millennials Now Reject Capitalism, Poll Shows." *The Washington Post*, April 26, 2016. https://www.washingtonpost.com/news/wonk/wp/2016/04/26/a-majority-of-millennials-now-reject-capitalism-poll-shows/.

Fraser Institute. "Economic Freedom of the World: 2020 Annual Report." Accessed January 29, 2021. https://www.fraserinstitute.org/studies/economic-freedom-of-the-world-2020-annual-report.

Friedman, Milton. "A Friedman doctrine - The Social Responsibility of Business Is to Increase Its Profits." *The New York Times,* September 13, 1970. https://www.nytimes.com/1970/09/13/archives/a-friedman-doctrine-the-social-responsibility-of-business-is-to.html.

Foroohar, Rana. *Makers and Takers: The Rise of Finance and the Fall of American Business.* Crown Business, 2016.

Garden, Jenna. "Rose Marcario: Environmentalism Is for Everyone." *Insights by Stanford Business*, June 1, 2020. https://www.gsb.stanford.edu/insights/rose-marcario-environmentalism-everyone.

Hong, Limei. "Patagonia's Circular Economy Strategy." *Business of Fashion,* January 17, 2017. https://www.businessoffashion.com/articles/sustainability/how-patagonia-transformed-the-circular-economy.

Marcario, Rose. "Patagonia CEO: This Is Why We're Suing President Trump." *Time*, December 6, 2017. https://time.com/5052617/patagonia-ceo-suing-donald-trump/.

Marcario, Rose. "Sand Mandalas & Goodbyes." *LinkedIn*, June 17, 2020. https://www.linkedin.com/pulse/sand-mandalas-goodbyes-rose-marcario/.

MIT Sloan. "How These Leading CEOs Use Questions to Drive Success." November 8, 2018. https://mitsloan.mit.edu/ideas-made-to-matter/how-these-leading-ceos-use-questions-to-drive-success.

Parker, Kim, Rachel Minkin, and Jesse Bennett. "Economic Fallout From COVID-19 Continues to Hit Lower-Income Americans the Hardest." *Pew Research Center*, September 24, 2020. https://www.pewsocialtrends.org/2020/09/24/economic-fallout-from-covid-19-continues-to-hit-lower-income-americans-the-hardest/.

Patagonia. "100 Percent Today, 1 Percent Every Day." Accessed January 29, 2021. https://www.patagonia.ca/stories/100-percent-today-1-percent-every-day/story-31099.html.

Patagonia. "Record-Breaking Black Friday Sales to Benefit the Planet." Accessed January 29, 2021. http://www.patagoniaworks.com/press/2016/12/8/record-breaking-black-friday-sales-to-benefit-the-planet.

Saad, Lydia. "Socialism as Popular as Capitalism Among Young Adults in U.S." *Gallup*, November 25, 2019. https://news.gallup.com/poll/268766/socialism-popular-capitalism-among-young-adults.aspx.

CHAPTER 2

Coleman, Joshua. "What Boomers Can Learn from Millennials about Changing the World — and Their Relationships," NBC News, March 2, 2021. https://www.nbcnews.com/think/opinion/what-boomers-can-learn-millennials-about-changing-world-your-relationships-ncna1259290.

Earth Observatory. "World of Change: Global Temperatures." Accessed January 29, 2021. https://earthobservatory.nasa.gov/world-of-change/global-temperatures.

Encyclopedia Britannica Online, Academic ed., s.v. "Robert Owen."

Accessed January 29, 2021. https://www.britannica.com/biography/Robert-Owen.

"Munich Re Analyzes Katrina/Rita Impact; Insured Loss Around $40 Billion." *Insurance Journal*, September 28, 2005. https://www.insurancejournal.com/news/international/2005/09/28/60241.htm.

PWC. "Will Robots Really Steal Our Jobs?" https://www.pwc.co.uk/economic-services/assets/international-impact-of-automation-feb-2018.pdf.

UNESCO. "Women in Science, Fact Sheet No 55," June 2019. http://uis.unesco.org/sites/default/files/documents/fs55-women-in-science-2019-en.pdf.

World Economic Forum. "The Future of Jobs Report 2020." October 20, 2020. https://www.weforum.org/reports/the-future-of-jobs-report-2020/in-full/infographics-e4e69e4de7.

World Economic Forum. "The Global Gender Gap Report 2018," 2018. http://www3.weforum.org/docs/WEF_GGGR_2018.pdf.

CHAPTER 3

Brené Brown. "Dare to Lead." Accessed January 29, 2021. https://daretolead.brenebrown.com/.

Brown, Brené. *Dare to Lead: Brave Work. Tough Conversations. Whole Hearts.* Read by Brené Brown. Random House Audio, 2018. Audible audio ed.

Entrepreneur. "Anita Roddick." October 10, 2008. https://www.entrepreneur.com/article/197688.

Fowler, Susan. "Reflecting on One Very, Very Strange Year at Uber." *Susan Fowler* (blog), February 19, 2017. https://www.susanjfowler.com/blog/2017/2/19/reflecting-on-one-very-strange-year-at-uber.

Fridays for the Future. "Homepage." Accessed January 29, 2021. https://fridaysforfuture.org/

Friedman, Zack. "Understand This Before You #DeleteUber." *Forbes*, February 1, 2017. https://www.forbes.com/sites/zack-friedman/2017/02/01/uber-lyft/?sh=19189d8d61c3.

Gajanan, Mahita. "You Have Stolen My Dreams and My Childhood: Grete Thunberg Gives Powerful Speech at UN Climate Summit." *Time*, September 23, 2019. https://time.com/5684216/greta-thunberg-un-climate-action-summit-climate-speech/.

Grant, Adam. "In Negotiations, Givers Are Smarter Than Takers." *The New York Times*, March 27, 2020. https://www. nytimes.com/2020/03/27/smarter-living/negotiation-tips-giver-taker.html.

Grant, Adam. *Give and Take: A Revolutionary Approach to Success.* Read by Brian Keith Lewis. Penguin Audio, 2013. Audible audio ed.

Kalanick, Travis. "Standing up for What's Right." *Facebook*, January 28, 2017. https://www.facebook.com/traviskal/posts/1331814113506421.

Larcker, David and Brian Tayan. "Governance Gone Wild: Epic Misbehavior at Uber Technologies." *Stanford Closer Look Series*, October 11, 2017. https://www.gsb.stanford.edu/sites/default/files/publication-pdf/cgri-closer-look-70-governance-gone-wild-uber-technologies.pdf.

Swisher, Kara and Bhuiyan, Johana. "Uber CEO Kalanick Advised Employees on Sex Rules for a Company Celebration in 2013 'Miami Letter.'" *Vox,* June 8, 2017. https://www.vox.com/2017/6/8/15765514/2013-miami-letter-uber-ceo-kalanick-employees-sex-rules-company-celebration.

Wakabayashi, Daisuke and Mike Isaac. "Google Self-Driving Car Unit Accuses Uber of Using Stolen Technology." *The New York Times*, February 23, 201. https://nyti.ms/2lBg6jZ.

CHAPTER 4

Allianz. "Ethics and investing: How Environmental, Social, and Governance Issues Impact Investor Behavior." https://www.allianzlife.com/-/media/files/allianz/pdfs/esg-white-paper.pdf.

Amaren, Swetha. "What Are Your Customers' Expectations for Social Media Response Time?" *Hubspot*. Accessed January 29, 2021. https://blog.hubspot.com/service/social-media-response-time.

Coldwell Banker. "A Look at Wealth 2019: Millennial Millionaires." October 16, 2019. https://blog.coldwellbankerluxury.com/wp-content/uploads/2019/10/CBGL-Millennial-Report_SEP19_FINAL-4a.1-1-1.pdf.

Conners, Leila, and Nadia Conners, dir. The 11th Hour. 2009.

Cowen, Tyler. "The Marriages of Power Couples Reinforce Income Inequality." *The New York Times,* December 14, 2015. https://www.nytimes.com/2015/12/27/upshot/marriages-of-power-er-couples-reinforce-income-inequality.html?_r=1.

Davis, Nicola. "Kofi Annan: We Must Challenge Climate-Change Sceptics Who Deny the Facts." *The Guardian*, May 3, 2015. https://www.theguardian.com/environment/2015/may/03/kofi-annan-interview-climate-change-paris-summit-sceptics.

Edelman. "Two-Thirds of Consumers Worldwide Now Buy on Beliefs." Accessed January 29, 2021. www.edelman.com/news-awards/two-thirds-consumers-worldwide-now-buy-beliefs.

Global Impact Investing Network. "What You Need to Know About Impact Investing." Accessed January 29, 2021. https://thegiin. org/impact-investing/need-to-know/#how-big-is-the-impact-investing-market.

Hanauer, Nick and David Rolf. "The Top 1% of Americans Have Taken $50 Trillion From the Bottom 90%—And That's Made the U.S. Less Secure." *Time*, September 14, 2020. https://time. com/5888024/50-trillion-income-inequality-america/.

Ho, Sally. "Conscious Consumers: 10 Ways Millennials & Gen Zs Are Changing How & What We Buy." *Green Queen*, July 10, 2020. https://www.greenqueen.com.hk/10-ways-millennials-gen-zs-are-changing-what-and-how-we-buy-conscious-consumers/

IPCC. "Understanding Global Warming of 1.5°C." Accessed January 29, 2021. https://www.ipcc.ch/sr15/.

Kelly, Jack. "Millennials Will Become Richest Generation in American History as Baby Boomers Transfer Over Their Wealth." *Forbes*, October 26, 2019. https://www.forbes.com/sites/jack-kelly/2019/10/26/millennials-will-become-richest-generation-in-american-history-as-baby-boomers-transfer-over-th eir-wealth/#1381ce046c4b.

Manyika, James, Susan Lund, Michael Chui, Jacques Bughin, Jonathan Woetzel, Parul Batra, Ryan Ko, and Saurabh Sanghvi. "Jobs Lost, Jobs Gained: What the future of work will mean for jobs, skills, and wages." *McKinsey & Company*, November 28, 2017. https://www.mckinsey.com/featured-insights/future-of-work/jobs-lost-jobs-gained-what-the-future-of-work-will-mean-for-jobs-skills-and-wages.

Meredith, Sam. "Sustainable Investment Funds Just Surpassed $1 Trillion for the First Time on Record." *CNBC*, August 11, 2020. https://www.cnbc.com/2020/08/11/coronavirus-esg-and-sustainable-funds-surpass-1-trillion-for-the-first-time.html.

Metz, Neil and Maria Burdina. "How Neighborhood Inequality Leads to Higher Crime Rates." *LSE*. Accessed January 29, 2021. https://blogs.lse.ac.uk/usappblog/2016/07/08/how-neighborhood-inequality-leads-to-higher-crime-rates/.

Obama White House Archives. "Remarks by the President at UN Climate Change Summit." September 23, 2014. https://obamawhitehouse.archives.gov/the-press-office/2014/09/23/remarks-president-un-climate-change-summit.

Price, Carter and Kathryn A. Edwards. "Trends in Income From 1975 to 2018." *Rand Corporation*. Accessed January 29, 2021. https://www.rand.org/pubs/working_papers/WRA516-1.html.

Sehl, Katie. "Top Twitter Demographics That Matter to Social Media Marketers." *Hootsuite*, May 28, 2020. https://blog.hootsuite.com/twitter-demographics/.

Stock, Kyle. "Sunday Strategist: CrossFit Isn't Canceled, But It's Close." *Bloomberg*, June 14, 2020. https://www.bloomberg.com/news/newsletters/2020-06-14/crossfit-crisis-is-a-good-example-of-the-founder-s-dilemma.

The Economist. "The stark relationship between income inequality and crime." June 7, 2018. https://www.economist.com/graphic-detail/2018/06/07/the-stark-relationship-between-income-inequality-and-crime.

The World Bank Database (accessed January 29, 2021). https://data.
worldbank.org/indicator/NY.GDP.MKTP.CD?locations=CN.

University of Michigan. "Rising Wealth Inequality: Causes, Consequences and Potential Responses. "Accessed January 29, 2021.
https://poverty.umich.edu/research-projects/policy-briefs/
rising-wealth-inequality-causes-consequences-and-poten-
tial-responses/.

Viens, Ashley. "This Graph Tells Us Who's Using Social Media the
Most." *World Economic Forum*, October 2019. https://www.
weforum.org/agenda/2019/10/social-media-use-by-generation/.

CHAPTER 5
Chowdhry, Amit. "Microsoft Monday: Satya Nadella's 'Hit Refresh,'
Office 2019, Microsoft Windows Store Gets Rebranded."
Forbes, October 2, 2017. https://www.forbes.com/sites/
amitchowdhry/2017/10/02/microsoft-monday-satya-nadel-
las-hit-refresh-office-2019-microsoft-windows-store-gets-re-
branded/?sh=19e9da8c2726.

Crowley, Richie. "Jack Dorsey on Mindfulness in Under 2 Minutes."
Medium (blog), May 28, 2020. https://rickieticklez.medium.
com/jack-dorsey-on-mindfulness-in-under-2-minutes-
41b5e0dc342d.

Frankl, Viktor. *Man's Search for Meaning.* Boston: Beacon Press,
2006.

Hao. "Bob Iger: Daily Routine." *Balance the Grind*, August 16, 2020. https://www.balancethegrind.com.au/daily-routines/bob-iger-daily-routine/.

Iger, Robert. *The Ride of a Lifetime: Lessons Learned From 15 Years as CEO of the Walt Disney Company*. Read by Jim Frangione and Robert Iger. Random House Audio, 2019. Audible audio ed.

Klein, Ezra. "Yuval Harari, Author of *Sapiens*, on How Meditation Made Him a Better Historian," *Vox*. February 28, 2017. https://www.vox.com/2017/2/28/14745596/yuval-harari-sapiens-interview-meditation-ezra-klein.

Nadella, Satya. *Hit Refresh: The Quest to Rediscover Microsoft's Soul and Imagine a Better Future for Everyone*. Read by Shridhar Solanki and Satya Nadella. Harper Audio, 2017. Audible audio ed.

Neurohealth. "Brainwaves the Language." Accessed January 25, 2021. https://nhahealth.com/brainwaves-the-language/.

Stillman, Jessica. "This 5-Second Morning Ritual Sets Satya Nadella Up for All-Day Success," *Inc.*, June 17, 2020. https://www.inc.com/jessica-stillman/this-5-second-morning-ritual-sets-satya-nadella-up-for-all-day-success.html#:~.

CHAPTER 6

Allan, David G. "The Google Engineer Teaching Happiness in three Steps." *BBC Future*, November 10, 2014. https://www.bbc.com/future/article/20141110-googles-algorithm-for-happiness.

Baer, Drake. "Here's What Google Teaches Employees in Its Search Inside Yourself Course." *Business Insider*, August 5, 2014. https://www.businessinsider.com/search-inside-your-self-googles-life-changing-mindfulness-course-2014-8.

Chade-Meng. "About Meng-Bio." Accessed January 24, 2021. http://chademeng.com/about/.

Draznin, Haley. "Eileen Fisher Built a Fashion Empire. Her Employees Now Own Nearly Half of It." *CNN Business*, January 6, 2020. https://edition.cnn.com/2020/01/06/success/eileen-fisher-profit-sharing-fashion-boss-files/index.html.

Eileen Fisher, Inc. "Company Overview." Accessed January 24, 2020. https://www.eileenfisher.com/company-overview.

Eileen Fisher, Inc. "Environmental Justice Grant." Accessed January 24, 2020. https://www.eileenfisher.com/environmental-justice-grant.

Kelly, Caitlin. "OK, Google, Take a Deep Breath." *The New York Times*, April 28, 2012. https://www.nytimes.com/2012/04/29/technology/google-course-asks-employees-to-take-a-deep-breath.html.

Klemp, Nate. "5 Reasons Your Company Should be Investing in Mindfulness Training." *Inc.*, October 17, 2019. https://www.inc.com/nate-klemp/5-reasons-your-company-should-be-in-vesting-in-mindfulness-training.html.

Tenney, Matt. "Be a 'Don't Knower': One of Eileen Fisher's Secrets to Success," *Huffington Post*, May 15, 2015. https://www.huffpost.com/entry/be-a-dont-knower-one-of-e_b_7242468.

UC Davis Health Medical Center. "Gratitude Is Good Medicine." November 25, 2015. https://health.ucdavis.edu/medicalcenter/features/2015-2016/11/20151125_gratitude.html#.

CHAPTER 7

Anderson, John R. *Cognitive Psychology and Its Implications* (New York: Worth Publishers, 2010), 153.

Cherry, Kendra. "The Role of a Schema in Psychology," *Very Well Mind*, September 23, 2019. https://www.verywellmind.com/what-is-a-schema-2795873.

Gallo, Amy. "How to Build the Social Ties You Need at Work," *Harvard Business Review*, September 23, 2015. https://hbr.org/2015/09/how-to-build-the-social-ties-you-need-at-work.

Gruber, Matthias J., and Charan Ranganath. "How Curiosity Enhances Hippocampus-Dependent Memory: The Prediction, Appraisal, Curiosity, and Exploration (PACE) Framework," *Trends in Cognitive Sciences*, November 6, 2019. https://www.cell.com/trends/cognitive-sciences/fulltext/S1364-6613(19)30238-4.

Hershey Story. "The Man Behind the Chocolate Bar." Accessed February 23, 2021. https://hersheystory.org/wp-content/uploads/2015/06/Milton-Hershey-The-Man-Behind-The-Chocolate.pdf.

Hoffman, W. Michael, Robert E. Frederick, and Mark S. Schwartz. *Business Ethics: Readings and Cases in Corporate Morality (5th ed)*, (John Wiley & Sons, Inc., 2014).

Kashdan, Todd B. and John E. Roberts. "Trait and State Curiosity in the Genesis of Intimacy: Differentiation from Related Constructs." *Guildford Press Periodicals*, June 2005. https://guilfordjournals.com/doi/pdf/10.1521/jscp.23.6.792.54800.

Kashdan, Todd B., Ryne A. Sherman, Jessica Yarbro, and David C. Funder. "How Are Curious People Viewed and How Do They Behave in Social Situations? From the Perspectives of Self, Friends, Parents, and Unacquainted Observers." *Wiley Online Library*, May 15, 2012. https://onlinelibrary.wiley.com/doi/full/10.1111/j.1467-6494.2012.00796.x.

Karelaia, Natalia. "When in Doubt, Leaders Should Ask Questions," *INSEAD*. March 9, 2020. https://knowledge.insead.edu/leadership-organisations/when-in-doubt-leaders-should-ask-questions-13501.

Le Cunff, Anne-Laure. "Confirmation Bias: Believing What You See, Seeing What You Believe." *Ness Labs*. Accessed February 22, 2021. https://nesslabs.com/confirmation-bias.

Merck. "2020 State of Curiosity Report: Survey Analyzes the Curiosity of Merck Employees." January 28, 2021. https://www.merckgroup.com/en/news/2020-state-of-curiosity-report-28-01-2021.html.

Merck. "Merck Named a Global Top Employer." February 6, 2019. https://www.merckgroup.com/en/news/global-top-employer-2019-06-02-2019.html#.

Weiss, Stephanie and David Bollier. "Merck & Company, Inc.: Having the Vision to Succeed." *St Andrew University.* Accessed January 29, 2021. https://www.andrews.edu/~tidwell/bsad560/Case-Merck.html.

Whatley, Mary. "The Benefits of Maintaining a Curious Mind in Older Age," *Psychology in Action*, February 20, 2020. https://www.psychologyinaction.org/psychology-in-action-1/2020/2/20/the-benefits-of-maintaining-a-curious-mind-in-older-age.

Young, Emma. "River blindness breakthrough offers new hope." *New Scientist*, March 7, 2002. https://www.newscientist.com/article/dn2016-river-blindness-breakthrough-offers-new-hope/.

CHAPTER 8

Ahmed, Waqas. "This Is the Indispensable Skill That Will Future-Proof Your Career." *Fast Company*, June 16, 2020. https://www.fastcompany.com/90516784/this-is-the-indispensable-skill-that-will-future-proof-your-career.

Catmull, Ed. "How Pixar Fosters Collective Creativity." *Harvard Business Review*, September 2008. https://hbr.org/2008/09/how-pixar-fosters-collective-creativity.

Deloitte. "The Collaborative Economy." 2014. https://www2.deloitte. com/content/dam/Deloitte/au/Documents/Economics/deloit- te-au-economics-collaborative-economy-google-170614.pdf.

Magnusson, KR and BL Brim, "The Aging Brain." *Reference Module in Biomedical Sciences*, 2014.

Office Snapshots. "Pixar Headquarters and the Legacy of Steve Jobs." Accessed February 28, 2021. https://officesnapshots. com/2012/07/16/pixar-headquarters-and-the-legacy-of-steve- jobs/.

Taylor, William C. and Polly Labarre. "How Pixar Adds a New School of Thought to Disney." *The New York Times*, January 29, 2006. https://www.nytimes.com/2006/01/29/business/your- money/how-pixar-adds-a-new-school-of-thought-to-disney. html.

Verdolin, Jennifer. "3 Ways to Improve Your Cognitive Flex- ibility." *Psychology Today*, December 3, 2019. https:// www.psychologytoday.com/intl/blog/wild-connec- tions/201912/3-ways-improve-your-cognitive-flexibility.

CHAPTER 9

ATP Tour (blog). "Federer: 'I'm Not an Artist or A Musician.'" Jan- uary 20, 2020. https://www.atptour.com/en/news/federer-reac- tion-australian-open-2019-monday.

Medtronic Labs. "About." Accessed February 7, 2021. https://www. mdtlabs.org/about.

Medtronic Labs. "Medtronic Labs FY20 Impact Report." Accessed February 26, 2021. https://static1.squarespace.com/static/5e42f-21345fe7a57b627fe2f/t/5f341ba729e87554ceecee2e/1597250475474/FY20_Impact+Report.pdf.

CHAPTER 10

Albert-Deitch, Cameron. "Comfy Shoes Helped Allbirds Become a $1.4 Billion Company, but It's Never Been Just About Shoes." *Inc.*, December 4, 2018. https://www.inc.com/cameron-al-bert-deitch/allbirds-2018-company-of-the-year-nominee.html.

Albert-Deitch, Cameron. "A Decade Ago, He Helped Lead New Zealand to the World Cup. Now, Allbirds's Founder Is Bring-ing Those Team-Building Lessons to His Company." *Inc.*, Sep-tember 17, 2019. https://www.inc.com/cameron-albert-deitch/allbirds-tim-brown-company-culture-pro-sports.html.

Allbirds. "Sustainability." Accessed March 3, 2021. https://www.allbirds.com/pages/sustainability.

Boynton, Andy. "Unilever's Paul Polman: CEOs Can't Be Slaves to Shareholders." *Forbes*, July 20, 2015. https://www.forbes.com/sites/andyboynton/2015/07/20/unilevers-paul-polman-ceos-cant-be-slaves-to-shareholders/?sh=564b9407561e.

Buckland, Jason. "Tim Brown on Co-CEOs at Allbirds, and Leav-ing No Carbon Footprint Behind." *ShopifyPlus*, January 5, 2021.

https://www.shopify.com/enterprise/tim-brown-on-co-ceos-
at-allbirds-and-leaving-no-carbon-footprint-behind.

Catmull, Ed. "How Pixar Fosters Collective Creativity." *Harvard
Business Review*, September 2008. https://hbr.org/2008/09/
how-pixar-fosters-collective-creativity.

Cunningham, Lilian. "The Tao of Paul Polman." *The Washington
Post*. May 21, 2015. https://www.washingtonpost.com/news/
on-leadership/wp/2015/05/21/the-tao-of-paul-polman/.

Gelles, David. "He Ran an Empire of Soap and Mayonnaise. Now
He Wants to Reinvent Capitalism." *New York Times*, August 29,
2019. https://www.nytimes.com/2019/08/29/business/paul-pol-
man-unilever-corner-office.html.

Gelles, David. "Paul Polman, a 'Crucial Voice' for Corporate
Responsibility, Steps Down as Unilever C.E.O." *New York Times*,
November 29, 2018. https://www.nytimes.com/2018/11/29/busi-
ness/unilever-ceo-paul-polman.html.

London, Lela. "Allbirds Is the First Fashion Brand to Label Its
Carbon Footprint Like Calories." *Forbes*. April 15, 2020. https://
www.forbes.com/sites/lelalondon/2020/04/15/allbirds-is-the-
first-fashion-brand-to-label-its-carbon-footprint-like-calo-
ries/?sh=5acbaea070db.

Polman, Paul. "Without Collective Action None of Us Will Make It
to the Top." *LinkedIn*, February 19, 2018. https://www.linkedin.
com/pulse/without-collective-action-none-us-make-top-paul-
polman.

Schwartz, Evan. "Anchoring OKRs to Your Mission." *What Matters,* June 26, 2019. https://www.whatmatters.com/articles/okrs-mission-statement-allbirds-sustainability/.

Unilever. "Healthy Handwashing Habits for Life." Accessed February 26, 2021. https://www.unilever.com/sustainable-living/improving-health-and-well-being/health-and-hygiene/healthy-handwashing-habits-for-life/.

Unilever. "Lessons Learnt: Visibility Leads to Sustainable Sourcing." Accessed February 26, 2021. https://www.unilever.com/news/news-and-features/Feature-article/2020/lessons-learnt-visibility-leads-to-sustainable-sourcing.html.

Unilever. "Sustainable Living." Accessed February 7, 2021. https://www.unilever.com/sustainable-living/.

Unilever. "Unilever Aims to Double Business, Whilst Reducing Environmental Footprint." Accessed February 7, 2021. https://www.unilever.com/news/press-releases/2010/10-02-25-Unilever-aims-to-double-business-whilst-reducing-environmental-footprint.html.

Unilever. "Unilever CEO Announcement: Paul Polman to Retire; Alan Jope Appointed as Successor." November 29, 2018. https://www.unilever.com/news/press-releases/2018/unilever-ceo-announcement.html.

Unilever. "Unilever's Purpose-Led Brands Outperform." June 11, 2019. https://www.unilever.com/news/press-releases/2019/unilevers-purpose-led-brands-outperform.html.

CHAPTER 11

Clear, James. "Continuous Improvement: How It Works and How to Master It." *James Clear* (blog). Accessed March 1, 2021. https://jamesclear.com/continuous-improvement#:~:-text=Here's%20the%20punchline%3A,up%20over%20the%20long%2Dterm.

World Economic Forum. "Measuring Stakeholder Capitalism: Toward Common Metrics and Consistent Reporting of Sustainable Value Creation." September 2020. http://www3.weforum.org/docs/WEF_IBC_Measuring_Stakeholder_Capitalism_Report_2020.pdf.

World Economic Forum. "The Future of the Corporation: Moving from Balance Sheet to Value Sheet." January 2021. http://www3.weforum.org/docs/WEF_The_Future_of_the_Corporation_2021.pdf.

Printed in Poland
by Amazon Fulfillment
Poland Sp. z o.o., Wrocław